Anonymus

Local Government Board for Ireland

Sixteenth report

Anonymus

Local Government Board for Ireland
Sixteenth report

ISBN/EAN: 9783742811202

Manufactured in Europe, USA, Canada, Australia, Japa

Cover: Foto ©Suzi / pixelio.de

Manufactured and distributed by brebook publishing software
(www.brebook.com)

Anonymus

Local Government Board for Ireland

ANNUAL REPORT

OF

THE LOCAL GOVERNMENT BOARD FOR IRELAND,

BEING

THE SIXTEENTH REPORT UNDER "THE LOCAL GOVERNMENT BOARD (IRELAND) ACT," 35 & 36 VIC., c. 69.

Presented to both Houses of Parliament by Command of Her Majesty.

DUBLIN:
PRINTED FOR HER MAJESTY'S STATIONERY OFFICE
BY
ALEXANDER THOM & CO. (LIMITED),
And to be purchased, either directly or through any Bookseller, from
EYRE and SPOTTISWOODE, East Harding-street, Fetter-lane, E.C., or 88, Abingdon-street, Westminster, S.W.; or ADAM and CHARLES BLACK, 6, North Bridge, Edinburgh; or HODGES, FIGGIS, and Co., 104, Grafton-street, Dublin.

1888

TABLE OF CONTENTS.

A 2

APPENDIX.

APPENDIX A.—Orders, Circulars, and Correspondence, under the Poor Law Acts and other Acts not included in Appendix B or C.

I.—Orders.

II. Circulars.

III.—Correspondence.

Dissolution of Boards of Guardians.

APPENDIX B.—Medical Charities Act and Vaccination Acts.

APPENDIX E.—Tabular Returns in connexion with Relief under the Medical Charities Act.

ANNUAL REPORT

OF THE

LOCAL GOVERNMENT BOARD FOR IRELAND,

BEING THE

SIXTEENTH REPORT UNDER "THE LOCAL GOVERNMENT BOARD (IRELAND) ACT," 35 & 36 VIC., CAP. 69.

TO HIS EXCELLENCY CHARLES STEWART, MARQUIS OF LONDONDERRY, K.G., &c., &c., &c.,

Lord Lieutenant General and General Governor of Ireland.

Local Government Board,
Dublin, 10*th May*, 1888.

MAY IT PLEASE YOUR EXCELLENCY,

WE, the Local Government Board for Ireland, submit to your Excellency this our Sixteenth Annual Report under the Statute 35 & 36 Vic., cap. 69, entitled "The Local Government Board (Ireland) Act, 1872," relating to our proceedings up to the 31st March, 1888.

POOR RELIEF.

1. We submit, in the first place, in continuation of similar returns in previous Annual Reports, summaries of weekly returns showing the number of persons in receipt of relief, in the workhouses and out of the workhouses, at the close of each of the fifty-two weeks from the week ended 5th February, 1887, to the week ended 28th January, 1888, both inclusive; and we annex two diagrams,* in illustration of these and previous returns, showing the fluctuations which have occurred from week to week in the number of workhouse inmates and the number of persons in receipt of out-door relief, respectively, during the year terminated on the latter date and each of the six preceding years.

* Facing page 88.

STATEMENT, compiled from Weekly Returns, showing the number of Persons ended 5th February, 1887, to the week

Week ended Saturday.	Relief in Workhouses.																		
	Able-bodied.			Children under 15 years of age.	Sick in Workhouse Hospitals.			All other Classes.			Total Number in Workhouses.	Average Weekly Cost per head for Provisions, Necessaries, and Clothing.	Deaths.		No. of Persons ...				
	Males.	Females.	Total.		Fever Patients.	Other Cases.	Total.	Males aged 15 and upwards.	Females aged 15 and upwards.	Total.			No. in the Week.	Weekly Rate of Mortality per 1,000.	[illegible]	[illegible]	Fever Cases.	Other Cases.	Total.
1886.												s. d.							
Feb.	[illegible]	[illegible]	[illegible]	[illegible]	[illegible]	[illegible]	[illegible]	[illegible]	[illegible]	[illegible]	[illegible]	[illegible]	[illegible]	[illegible]	[illegible]	[illegible]	[illegible]	[illegible]	[illegible]
Mar.	[illegible]	[illegible]	[illegible]	[illegible]	[illegible]	[illegible]	[illegible]	[illegible]	[illegible]	[illegible]	[illegible]	[illegible]	[illegible]	[illegible]	[illegible]	[illegible]	[illegible]	[illegible]	[illegible]
April	[illegible]	[illegible]	[illegible]	[illegible]	[illegible]	[illegible]	[illegible]	[illegible]	[illegible]	[illegible]	[illegible]	[illegible]	[illegible]	[illegible]	[illegible]	[illegible]	[illegible]	[illegible]	[illegible]
May	[illegible]	[illegible]	[illegible]	[illegible]	[illegible]	[illegible]	[illegible]	[illegible]	[illegible]	[illegible]	[illegible]	[illegible]	[illegible]	[illegible]	[illegible]	[illegible]	[illegible]	[illegible]	[illegible]
June	[illegible]	[illegible]	[illegible]	[illegible]	[illegible]	[illegible]	[illegible]	[illegible]	[illegible]	[illegible]	[illegible]	[illegible]	[illegible]	[illegible]	[illegible]	[illegible]	[illegible]	[illegible]	[illegible]
July	[illegible]	[illegible]	[illegible]	[illegible]	[illegible]	[illegible]	[illegible]	[illegible]	[illegible]	[illegible]	[illegible]	[illegible]	[illegible]	[illegible]	[illegible]	[illegible]	[illegible]	[illegible]	[illegible]
Aug.	[illegible]	[illegible]	[illegible]	[illegible]	[illegible]	[illegible]	[illegible]	[illegible]	[illegible]	[illegible]	[illegible]	[illegible]	[illegible]	[illegible]	[illegible]	[illegible]	[illegible]	[illegible]	[illegible]
Sept.	[illegible]	[illegible]	[illegible]	[illegible]	[illegible]	[illegible]	[illegible]	[illegible]	[illegible]	[illegible]	[illegible]	[illegible]	[illegible]	[illegible]	[illegible]	[illegible]	[illegible]	[illegible]	[illegible]
Oct.	[illegible]	[illegible]	[illegible]	[illegible]	[illegible]	[illegible]	[illegible]	[illegible]	[illegible]	[illegible]	[illegible]	[illegible]	[illegible]	[illegible]	[illegible]	[illegible]	[illegible]	[illegible]	[illegible]
Nov.	[illegible]	[illegible]	[illegible]	[illegible]	[illegible]	[illegible]	[illegible]	[illegible]	[illegible]	[illegible]	[illegible]	[illegible]	[illegible]	[illegible]	[illegible]	[illegible]	[illegible]	[illegible]	[illegible]
Dec.	[illegible]	[illegible]	[illegible]	[illegible]	[illegible]	[illegible]	[illegible]	[illegible]	[illegible]	[illegible]	[illegible]	[illegible]	[illegible]	[illegible]	[illegible]	[illegible]	[illegible]	[illegible]	[illegible]
1887.																			
Jan.	[illegible]	[illegible]	[illegible]	[illegible]	[illegible]	[illegible]	[illegible]	[illegible]	[illegible]	[illegible]	[illegible]	[illegible]	[illegible]	[illegible]	[illegible]	[illegible]	[illegible]	[illegible]	[illegible]

in receipt of relief in Unions in Ireland, at the close of each week, from the week ended 28th January, 1888, both inclusive.

Included in the above admissions under the 1 Vic., c. 56, and sect. of 25 and 26			No. of Persons under treatment in Hospitals not connected with Workhouses, who have been sent there by the Guardians under sec. 11 of 6 & 7 Vic., c. 92, and of 25 & 26 Vic., c. 83.		No. of Blind and Deaf and Dumb persons maintained and instructed at the expense of the Poor Rates, and number of Idiots and Imbeciles maintained at the expense of the Poor Rates			Out-door Relief.									Total Number of Persons in receipt of Relief.
No. of Convalescent Patients under the 25th sec. of 25 & 26 Vic., c. 83.								Relievable under Section 1 of 10 Vic., cap. 31.		Relievable under 10 Vic., cap. 31, sect. 2, and sect. 1 of 11 & 12 Vic., c. 47, s. 4.		Under 25 & 26 Vic., c. 83. Number of Orphans and Deserted Children sent to Nurse.			Total Number of Persons in receipt of Out-door Relief.	
Fever Cases.	Other Cases.	Total.	In Fever Hospitals.	In other Hospitals.	Blind.	Deaf and Dumb.	Idiots and Imbeciles.	No. of Cases.	No. of Persons.	No. of Cases.	No. of Persons.	Male.	Female.	Total.		
[illegible]	[illegible]	[illegible]	[illegible]	[illegible]	[illegible]	[illegible]	[illegible]	[illegible]	[illegible]	[illegible]	[illegible]	[illegible]	[illegible]	[illegible]	[illegible]	[illegible]

2. The following tables show the maximum, minimum, and average daily number of persons in the workhouses and on out-door relief, respectively, during each of the seven years included in the diagrams:—

RELIEF IN WORKHOUSES.

—	Maximum Number.	Date.	Minimum Number.	Date.	Average Daily Number.
1881–82, .	58,505	12 February, 1881	47,183	10 September, 1881	52,772
1882–83, .	56,915	3 February, 1883	46,139	9 September, 1882	50,569
1883–84, .	54,645	17 February, 1883	44,216	15 September, 1883	49,236
1884–85, .	52,184	16 February, 1884	43,522	23 August, 1884	47,307
1885–86, .	50,426	7 February, 1885	42,250	29 August, 1885	46,163
1886–87, .	50,027	6 February, 1886	42,378	4 September, 1886	45,899
1887–88, .	49,403	5 February, 1887	42,225	6 August, 1887	45,536

OUT-DOOR RELIEF.

—	Maximum Number.	Date.	Minimum Number.	Date.	Average Daily Number.
1881–82, .	80,606	12 February, 1881	51,487	8 October, 1881	60,196
1882–83, .	64,041	5 February, 1883	53,556	14 October, 1882	58,833
1883–84, .	65,999	24 February, 1883	58,629	6 October, 1883	60,384
1884–85, .	61,579	22 March, 1884	53,537	11 October, 1884	57,819
1885–86, .	64,455	30 January, 1886	51,316	3 October, 1885	58,965
1886–87, .	162,428	29 May, 1886	59,845	2 October, 1886	78,241
1887–88, .	69,475	28 May, 1887	59,631	8 October, 1887	65,508

3. In our last Annual Report we drew attention to the fact that there was a decrease in the average daily number of persons relieved in the workhouses in the year ended January, 1887, as compared with the number so relieved in the preceding year.

We have now to report that the returns for the year just ended show a further decline in the average daily number of persons relieved in the workhouses. Your Excellency will observe that the average daily number of persons who received in-door relief in the year 1887-8 is less than the number so relieved in any of the other years included in the above table.

It will be seen from our former Report that the increase in the average daily number of persons relieved out of the workhouses in the year ended January, 1887, as compared with the previous year, was 19,270. This increase was, however, as stated, mainly due to the operation of the Poor Relief Act, 1886, which affected the returns for a period of fifteen weeks. The returns for the year just ended show a decrease of 12,733 in the average daily number of persons who received out-door relief as compared with the year ended January, 1887, above referred to. The number of persons so relieved is large as compared with other years included in the above table, and in the month of August last we thought it advisable to issue a circular to Boards of Guardians, a copy of which may be found in the Appendix,* on the subject of the remarkable increase which had taken place in that form of relief since it was first authorized by the passing of the Poor Relief Extension Act in the year 1847. In this circular we pointed

*See page 62.

out that from the year 1856 to the year 1885 the average daily number of persons in receipt of out-door relief had steadily increased from 926 to 56,434 (exclusive of the orphan and deserted children at nurse), while the annual cost of such relief had risen from £2,245 to £104,951, and, referring to the demoralizing tendency of this form of relief and the necessity for limiting it to cases of sickness and urgency, we suggested the season at which the circular was issued, viz., the autumn, to be a favourable time for the revision of the relief lists. The return given in the Table on page 3 shows a decline in the number of persons receiving out-door relief from the time of the issue of the circular referred to as compared with the corresponding period in the previous year, which period was not affected by the Poor Relief Act. The Poor Relief Act was in operation from the week ended 24th April to the week ended 31st July, and the following table shows the decrease in out-door relief in the last week of each month from August, 1887, to January, 1888, as compared with the year 1886–7.

4. Number of Persons in Workhouses and on Out-door Relief in the last week of each month during the Year ended 28th January, 1888, and in the corresponding weeks of the preceding year (ended 29th January, 1887).

Year 1887-8.				Year 1886-7.				Increase in the year 1887-8.		Decrease in the year 1887-8.	
	Number of Persons				Number of Persons						
Week ended	In Workhouses.	On Out-door Relief.	Total.	Week ended	In Workhouses.	On Out-door Relief.	Total.	In Workhouses.	On Out-door Relief.	In Workhouses.	On Out-door Relief.
1887.				**1886.**							
February 26,	43,931	67,095	108,726	February 27,	42,044	64,491	118,835	—	2,731	532	—
March 26,	44,104	68,108	112,310	March 27,	45,179	66,813	116,144	—	1,431	1,777	—
April 30,	45,777	69,797	110,561	April 24,	47,830	62,158	114,648	—	9,[illegible]	1,081	—
May 28,	41,309	68,473	114,883	May 22,	41,347	104,469	187,106	—	—	2,[illegible]	76,[illegible]
June 25,	42,331	68,871	111,730	June 26,	41,867	171,685	189,053	—	—	1,036	86,[illegible]
July 30,	44,715	67,151	109,486	July 31,	42,886	81,231	123,183	—	—	127	15,1[illegible]
August 27,	42,080	61,259	104,343	August 28,	41,907	62,351	104,871	177	—	—	78
September 24,	43,775	66,622	100,136	September 25,	42,466	61,394	104,730	659	—	—	871
October 29,	44,234	60,987	105,221	October 30,	43,860	61,779	104,618	446	—	—	895
November 26,	44,831	61,144	106,974	November 27,	43,931	62,477	106,498	561	—	—	76
December 31,	47,163	64,[illegible]	111,[illegible]	December 25,	47,016	64,151	111,110	449	—	—	1,460
1888.				**1887.**							
January 28,	43,871	60,048	114,319	January 29,	49,973	44,886	116,030	—	—	131	1,926

5. In our last Annual Report we alluded to the extravagant and inefficient manner in which certain Boards of Guardians in the west of Ireland had performed their duties in carrying out the provisions of the Poor Relief Act, 1886. In five of these Unions much financial embarrassment existed during the period embraced in this Report owing to the maladministration of the Guardians in the previous year, and these difficulties became so great in the Balmullet and Swinford Unions that we found it necessary, in pursuance of the powers vested in us by the 18th section of the Irish Poor Relief Extension Act, 10 Vic., cap. 31, to dissolve the Boards of Guardians and to place the management of these two Unions in the hands of paid officers.

The letter assigning our reason for this step in each case will be found in the Appendix.*

6. The following is a tabulated account of admissions to the workhouses during the year ended the 29th of September last, in comparison with those of the twenty-eight preceding years:—

Year ended 29th September.	Number of Paupers in Workhouses at the commencement of the Year.	Number of Persons admitted during the Year.						Number of Births in the Workhouses during the Year.	Total number of Persons relieved in the Workhouses during the Year.	Number of Deaths in the Workhouses during the Year.
		Number admitted in Sickness.				Number admitted who were not sick.	Total number of admissions during the Year.			
		Suffering from Fever or other contagious Disease.	Suffering under other Diseases.	Suffering from accidental Injury.	Total number admitted in Sickness.					
1859,	33,836	9,553	29,690	2,137	41,369	78,334	126,804	2,773	163,706	8,032
1860,	35,790	9,167	35,635	2,093	47,895	95,715	143,040	2,848	170,549	9,077
1861,	38,701	9,235	38,378	2,017	49,583	114,500	164,083	3,030	202,477	14,338
1862,	41,388	11,183	44,835	2,230	58,264	118,438	176,897	2,816	227,687	14,740
1863,	48,182	14,469	41,907	2,133	61,227	179,270	240,137	2,877	296,785	19,990
1864,	56,437	13,737	43,627	2,280	61,661	151,167	212,921	2,635	261,147	12,703
1865,	49,025	18,616	41,138	2,503	62,291	149,093	211,384	2,761	263,170	12,873
1866,	44,997	19,553	30,527	2,300	54,418	130,111	184,537	2,528	232,104	11,841
1867,	41,270	11,706	40,170	1,480	67,812	143,800	211,227	2,434	256,139	13,143
1868,	48,618	11,980	43,344	1,884	58,047	185,520	240,319	2,807	296,042	11,878
1869,	47,175	9,976	41,035	3,148	54,610	161,008	216,577	2,414	264,867	11,277
1870,	48,617	8,187	39,806	2,310	17,740	143,506	188,138	2,281	236,435	10,897
1871,	43,373	6,715	38,317	2,016	19,549	141,493	185,053	2,193	228,316	10,039
1872,	39,691	10,346	39,990	2,340	52,540	107,210	169,748	1,946	222,596	11,563
1873,	40,644	8,255	43,767	2,123	54,084	132,070	186,483	1,962	247,380	12,364
1874,	41,446	8,163	39,268	2,573	50,005	129,540	180,045	1,914	223,288	10,795
1875,	43,286	8,915	37,464	2,328	47,607	121,103	169,140	1,729	214,754	11,070
1876,	47,082	8,476	33,570	2,185	43,231	99,670	140,901	1,648	183,760	10,063
1877,	39,773	8,948	37,280	2,270	48,180	109,163	157,354	1,705	196,621	10,798
1878,	40,711	8,110	40,185	2,291	44,011	163,074	206,085	1,784	248,147	11,038
1879,	45,645	8,303	47,055	2,708	58,066	170,796	228,836	2,025	274,404	14,387
1880,	48,136	8,053	38,737	2,530	49,320	224,050	277,330	1,939	327,316	12,476
1881,	47,078	7,529	48,306	2,701	56,627	287,311	314,971	1,901	363,344	11,699
1882,	47,311	7,673	41,031	2,672	57,149	239,141	291,078	1,930	343,613	12,446
1883,	46,335	6,377	43,818	2,291	52,876	251,040	303,962	1,947	350,220	10,191
1884,	44,579	5,621	41,045	2,800	53,185	294,277	313,842	1,849	370,063	10,498
1885,	44,019	6,516	41,837	2,171	52,228	323,155	374,293	1,739	370,220	11,446
1886,	45,920	3,910	41,288	2,657	47,894	369,169	415,168	1,871	460,078	10,589
1887,	45,834	[illegible]	41,279	2,679	51,244	391,336	442,639	1,723	487,878	10,186

It will be observed from the above that there has been an increase of 3,248 in the total number admitted in sickness, and an increase of 23,396 in the number admitted who were not sick, thus showing an increase of 26,644 in the total number admitted during the year as compared with the previous year. The number suffering from fever or other contagious disease was greater by 257 than in the previous year, and the total number of persons relieved in workhouses shows an increase of 26,103.

* See pages 41 and 58.

7. The following is a statement of the result of the weekly summaries of in-door relief, showing the average daily number of recipients of relief for each of the thirty-three years ended 29th September, 1887:—

Average Daily Number in receipt of Relief during the year, Average Number of Deaths per Week, and Rate of Mortality.

Year ended 29th Sept.	Estimated Population.	Able-bodied.			[illegible]	Sick in Workhouse Hospitals.			All other Classes.			Total [illegible]	Deaths per Week.		[illegible]
		Males.	Females.	Total.		[illegible]	[illegible]	Total.	[illegible]	[illegible]	[illegible]		[illegible]	[illegible]	
1855,	[illegible]	[illegible]	14,[illegible]	18,134	[illegible]	[illegible]	18,314	[illegible]	[illegible]	[illegible]	7,[illegible]	78,511	[illegible]	3·5	1·30
1856,	[illegible]	[illegible]	[illegible]	14,264	[illegible]	1,218	16,[illegible]	17,[illegible]	[illegible]	[illegible]	7,10[illegible]	[illegible]	[illegible]	[illegible]	1·04
1857,	[illegible]	[illegible]	7,745	10,[illegible]	17,[illegible]	[illegible]	16,17[illegible]	16,440	[illegible]	4,1[illegible]	[illegible]	[illegible]	[illegible]	[illegible]	[illegible]
1858,	[illegible]	[illegible]	7,131	9,4[illegible]	14,[illegible]	1,168	[illegible]	[illegible]	[illegible]	4,[illegible]	[illegible]	[illegible]	[illegible]	[illegible]	0·78
1859,	[illegible]	[illegible]	[illegible]	7,754	11,311	874	[illegible]	14,[illegible]	[illegible]	4,[illegible]	[illegible]	40,[illegible]	[illegible]	[illegible]	0·67
1860,	[illegible]	[illegible]	[illegible]	7,037	11,316	[illegible]	13,[illegible]	14,[illegible]	2,115	[illegible]	7,[illegible]	41,[illegible]	[illegible]	[illegible]	0·60
1861,	[illegible]	[illegible]	[illegible]	[illegible]	12,[illegible]	1,[illegible]	14,[illegible]	[illegible]	[illegible]	[illegible]	[illegible]	46,1[illegible]	[illegible]	4·3	0·78
1862,	[illegible]	[illegible]	[illegible]	11,[illegible]	11,917	1,[illegible]	[illegible]	17,[illegible]	[illegible]	6,[illegible]	10,[illegible]	[illegible]	[illegible]	[illegible]	[illegible]
1863,	[illegible]	[illegible]	[illegible]	11,[illegible]	14,[illegible]	1,[illegible]	[illegible]	16,[illegible]	4,0[illegible]	[illegible]	11,[illegible]	67,[illegible]	[illegible]	4·1	1·01
1864,	[illegible]	[illegible]	7,670	10,[illegible]	16,176	1,[illegible]	10,[illegible]	18,[illegible]	4,[illegible]	[illegible]	11,[illegible]	66,[illegible]	914	4·3	[illegible]
1865,	[illegible]	[illegible]	4,647	[illegible]	[illegible]	1,[illegible]	[illegible]	[illegible]	[illegible]	[illegible]	11,[illegible]	[illegible]	[illegible]	4·2	[illegible]
1866,	[illegible]	[illegible]	[illegible]	[illegible]	14,[illegible]	1,[illegible]	[illegible]	17,[illegible]	4,411	[illegible]	[illegible]	[illegible]	[illegible]	[illegible]	[illegible]
1867,	[illegible]	[illegible]	[illegible]	[illegible]	16,[illegible]	1,[illegible]	15,[illegible]	[illegible]	[illegible]	[illegible]	11,[illegible]	[illegible]	[illegible]	[illegible]	[illegible]
1868,	[illegible]	[illegible]	[illegible]	[illegible]	[illegible]	[illegible]	[illegible]	[illegible]	[illegible]	7,[illegible]	[illegible]	[illegible]	[illegible]	4·1	[illegible]
1869,	[illegible]	[illegible]	[illegible]	[illegible]	[illegible]	[illegible]	[illegible]	16,[illegible]	[illegible]	[illegible]	12,[illegible]	[illegible]	[illegible]	4·1	[illegible]
1870,	[illegible]	[illegible]	[illegible]	7,[illegible]	13,[illegible]	[illegible]	16,[illegible]	[illegible]	[illegible]	[illegible]	[illegible]	[illegible]	[illegible]	4·1	[illegible]
1871,	[illegible]	[illegible]	[illegible]	[illegible]	[illegible]	[illegible]	[illegible]	[illegible]	[illegible]	[illegible]	[illegible]	[illegible]	[illegible]	[illegible]	[illegible]
1872,	[illegible]	[illegible]	[illegible]	[illegible]	11,[illegible]	[illegible]	15,[illegible]	16,[illegible]	[illegible]	[illegible]	[illegible]	[illegible]	[illegible]	[illegible]	[illegible]
1873,	[illegible]	[illegible]	[illegible]	[illegible]	12,[illegible]	[illegible]	15,[illegible]	[illegible]	[illegible]	[illegible]	[illegible]	[illegible]	[illegible]	[illegible]	[illegible]
1874,	[illegible]	[illegible]	[illegible]	[illegible]	11,[illegible]	[illegible]	15,[illegible]	[illegible]	[illegible]	[illegible]	[illegible]	[illegible]	[illegible]	4·1	[illegible]
1875,	[illegible]	[illegible]	[illegible]	[illegible]	[illegible]	[illegible]	[illegible]	16,[illegible]	[illegible]	[illegible]	[illegible]	[illegible]	[illegible]	[illegible]	[illegible]
1876,	[illegible]	[illegible]	4,1[illegible]	[illegible]	10,[illegible]	[illegible]	[illegible]	[illegible]	[illegible]	[illegible]	11,[illegible]	[illegible]	[illegible]	[illegible]	[illegible]
1877,	[illegible]	[illegible]	[illegible]	[illegible]	[illegible]	[illegible]	[illegible]	[illegible]	[illegible]	[illegible]	11,[illegible]	[illegible]	[illegible]	[illegible]	[illegible]
1878,	[illegible]	[illegible]	[illegible]	[illegible]	10,[illegible]	[illegible]	16,[illegible]	17,[illegible]	[illegible]	[illegible]	[illegible]	[illegible]	[illegible]	[illegible]	[illegible]
1879,	[illegible]	[illegible]	4,[illegible]	7,[illegible]	[illegible]	[illegible]	17,[illegible]	[illegible]	[illegible]	[illegible]	[illegible]	[illegible]	[illegible]	[illegible]	[illegible]
1880,	[illegible]	[illegible]	[illegible]	[illegible]	[illegible]	1,[illegible]	[illegible]	19,[illegible]	[illegible]	7,[illegible]	14,[illegible]	[illegible]	[illegible]	[illegible]	[illegible]
1881,	[illegible]	[illegible]	4,[illegible]	7,[illegible]	[illegible]	[illegible]	[illegible]	[illegible]	[illegible]	7,[illegible]	[illegible]	[illegible]	[illegible]	[illegible]	[illegible]
1882,	[illegible]	[illegible]	4,787	7,[illegible]	10,[illegible]	[illegible]	[illegible]	19,[illegible]	[illegible]	[illegible]	13,[illegible]	[illegible]	[illegible]	[illegible]	[illegible]
1883,	[illegible]	[illegible]	[illegible]	[illegible]	10,[illegible]	[illegible]	[illegible]	[illegible]	[illegible]	7,[illegible]	13,611	[illegible]	[illegible]	[illegible]	[illegible]
1884,	[illegible]	[illegible]	4,[illegible]	[illegible]	[illegible]	[illegible]	17,[illegible]	[illegible]	[illegible]	[illegible]	[illegible]	[illegible]	[illegible]	[illegible]	[illegible]
1885,	[illegible]	[illegible]	[illegible]	[illegible]	[illegible]	[illegible]	17,[illegible]	[illegible]	[illegible]	[illegible]	14,[illegible]	[illegible]	[illegible]	4·7	[illegible]
1886,	[illegible]	[illegible]	[illegible]	[illegible]	[illegible]	[illegible]	16,[illegible]	17,[illegible]	[illegible]	7,[illegible]	13,[illegible]	[illegible]	[illegible]	[illegible]	[illegible]
1887,	[illegible]	[illegible]	4,16[illegible]	[illegible]	[illegible]	[illegible]	16,[illegible]	[illegible]	[illegible]	[illegible]	[illegible]	[illegible]	[illegible]	[illegible]	[illegible]

6. We here continue from last Report a form of table exhibiting for the last thirty-five years the per-centage in each successive year of the several classes of workhouse inmates as compared with the whole number—

CLASSIFIED RETURN of the Number of Inmates of Workhouses in Ireland, on the first Saturday of January; and the per-centage of the several classes on the total Number of Inmates.

First Saturday of January.	Inmates not in Hospital.				Number in Hospital.	Total Number in Workhouses.	Per-centage on Total Number.				
	Able-bodied.		Children under 15 years of age.	Other classes.			Able-bodied.		Children under 15 years of age not in Hospital.	Other classes not in Hospital.	In Hospital.
	Male.	Female.					Male.	Female.			
7 Jan., 1854	9,290	11,864	[illegible]	8,180	[illegible]	[illegible]	6·6	[illegible]	49·6	8·1	[illegible]
6 " 1855	6,197	14,807	[illegible]	[illegible]	[illegible]	[illegible]	7·2	16·1	[illegible]	9·0	[illegible]
5 " 1856	[illegible]	[illegible]	[illegible]	7,717	[illegible]	72,341	6·4	18·0	37·7	[illegible]	[illegible]
3 " 1857	[illegible]	[illegible]	[illegible]	4,641	[illegible]	[illegible]	6·4	[illegible]	[illegible]	13·0	[illegible]
2 " 1858	[illegible]	[illegible]	[illegible]	[illegible]	[illegible]	[illegible]	[illegible]	[illegible]	31·7	[illegible]	[illegible]
1 " 1859	[illegible]	[illegible]	[illegible]	6,447	[illegible]	[illegible]	[illegible]	[illegible]	[illegible]	[illegible]	[illegible]
7 " 1860	[illegible]	6,101	11,707	[illegible]	[illegible]	43,316	6·1	15·7	27·1	17·4	34·7
5 " 1861	[illegible]	7,300	[illegible]	[illegible]	[illegible]	[illegible]	[illegible]	15·5	[illegible]	[illegible]	[illegible]
4 " 1862	[illegible]	[illegible]	[illegible]	[illegible]	[illegible]	[illegible]	[illegible]	16·7	[illegible]	[illegible]	[illegible]
3 " 1863	[illegible]	[illegible]	[illegible]	[illegible]	[illegible]	[illegible]	6·7	[illegible]	[illegible]	[illegible]	[illegible]
2 " 1864	[illegible]	[illegible]	[illegible]	[illegible]	[illegible]	[illegible]	[illegible]	[illegible]	[illegible]	[illegible]	[illegible]
7 " 1865	[illegible]	[illegible]	[illegible]	12,104	[illegible]	[illegible]	[illegible]	[illegible]	[illegible]	[illegible]	[illegible]
6 " 1866	[illegible]	[illegible]	[illegible]	[illegible]	[illegible]	[illegible]	[illegible]	[illegible]	[illegible]	21·1?	[illegible]
5 " 1867	3,016	[illegible]	[illegible]	[illegible]	[illegible]	[illegible]	[illegible]	[illegible]	[illegible]	[illegible]	[illegible]
4 " 1868	[illegible]	[illegible]	[illegible]	[illegible]	[illegible]	[illegible]	[illegible]	[illegible]	[illegible]	[illegible]	[illegible]
2 " 1869	[illegible]	[illegible]	[illegible]	[illegible]	19,019	[illegible]	[illegible]	15·4	[illegible]	[illegible]	[illegible]
1 " 1870	[illegible]	[illegible]	[illegible]	[illegible]	[illegible]	[illegible]	[illegible]	11·0?	[illegible]	[illegible]	[illegible]
7 " 1871	[illegible]	[illegible]	[illegible]	[illegible]	[illegible]	[illegible]	[illegible]	[illegible]	[illegible]	[illegible]	[illegible]
6 " 1872	[illegible]	[illegible]	[illegible]	[illegible]	[illegible]	[illegible]	[illegible]	[illegible]	[illegible]	[illegible]	[illegible]
4 " 1873	[illegible]	[illegible]	[illegible]	[illegible]	[illegible]	[illegible]	[illegible]	[illegible]	[illegible]	[illegible]	[illegible]
3 " 1874	[illegible]	[illegible]	13,165	[illegible]	[illegible]	[illegible]	[illegible]	[illegible]	[illegible]	[illegible]	[illegible]
2 " 1875	[illegible]	[illegible]	[illegible]	[illegible]	17,318	[illegible]	[illegible]	[illegible]	[illegible]	[illegible]	[illegible]
1 " 1876	[illegible]	[illegible]	[illegible]	[illegible]	[illegible]	[illegible]	[illegible]	[illegible]	[illegible]	[illegible]	[illegible]
6 " 1877	[illegible]	[illegible]	[illegible]	11,847	19,164	[illegible]	[illegible]	[illegible]	[illegible]	[illegible]	[illegible]
5 " 1878	[illegible]	[illegible]	[illegible]	[illegible]	[illegible]	[illegible]	[illegible]	[illegible]	[illegible]	[illegible]	[illegible]
4 " 1879	[illegible]	[illegible]	[illegible]	[illegible]	[illegible]	51,784?	[illegible]	[illegible]	[illegible]	[illegible]	[illegible]
3 " 1880	[illegible]	[illegible]	[illegible]	[illegible]	[illegible]	[illegible]	[illegible]	[illegible]	[illegible]	[illegible]	[illegible]
1 " 1881	[illegible]	[illegible]	[illegible]	[illegible]	[illegible]	[illegible]	[illegible]	[illegible]	[illegible]	[illegible]	[illegible]
7 " 1882	3,376	[illegible]	11,418?	[illegible]	[illegible]	53,781?	[illegible]	[illegible]	[illegible]	[illegible]	[illegible]
6 " 1883	[illegible]	6,141?	[illegible]	[illegible]	[illegible]	[illegible]	[illegible]	[illegible]	[illegible]	[illegible]	[illegible]
5 " 1884	[illegible]	[illegible]	[illegible]	[illegible]	[illegible]	[illegible]	[illegible]	[illegible]	[illegible]	[illegible]	[illegible]
3 " 1885	[illegible]	[illegible]	[illegible]	[illegible]	[illegible]	[illegible]	[illegible]	[illegible]	[illegible]	[illegible]	[illegible]
2 " 1886	[illegible]	[illegible]	[illegible]	[illegible]	[illegible]	[illegible]	[illegible]	[illegible]	[illegible]	[illegible]	[illegible]
1 " 1887	[illegible]	[illegible]	[illegible]	[illegible]	[illegible]	[illegible]	[illegible]	[illegible]	[illegible]	[illegible]	[illegible]
7 " 1888	[illegible]	[illegible]	[illegible]	[illegible]	[illegible]	[illegible]	[illegible]	[illegible]	[illegible]	[illegible]	[illegible]

9. We have subjoin a tabular statement showing the number of "night lodgers" (a term corresponding to "casuals" in England), from month to month, for the past twelve months, in continuation of a similar table in last Report.

RETURN of NIGHT-LODGERS, or CASUALS, relieved.

Week ended	Number relieved during the week.				Number in Workhouses at close of the week.				Number relieved in corresponding week of previous year.
	Males.	Females.	Children under 15.	Total.	Males.	Females.	Children under 15.	Total.	
5th March, 1887, .	3,562	664	677	4,903	474	104	85	663	3,793
2nd April, " .	3,616	745	708	5,069	484	87	80	651	4,129
7th May, " .	3,402	796	736	4,934	433	120	104	657	4,470
4th June, " .	3,511	867	738	5,116	431	141	100	672	4,559
2nd July, " .	1,931	575	491	2,997	291	54	76	421	3,633
6th August, " .	2,722	632	655	4,009	366	81	71	518	4,456
3rd September, " .	3,577	809	707	5,093	436	101	89	626	4,405
1st October, " .	3,759	846	706	4,975	410	134	85	629	4,605
5th November, " .	3,018	631	589	4,238	401	113	70	584	4,084
3rd December, " .	3,109	760	621	4,490	455	122	90	667	3,930
7th January, 1888, .	2,958	456	379	3,793	448	73	75	596	3,469
4th February, " .	3,701	611	440	4,752	474	160	71	645	4,433
3rd March, " .	3,813	597	477	4,877	471	96	84	651	4,903

There was a remarkable increase in the number of casuals relieved in the year ended March, 1887, as compared with the previous year, and, as stated in our last Report, we found from reports which we had obtained from our Inspectors that the increase was attributable, in a great measure, to applications for temporary relief in the workhouses from labourers and artisans, who, in consequence of want of employment in agricultural districts, and depression in trade, were travelling about the country seeking for employment. In the month of June last we issued a circular to Boards of Guardians, a copy of which may be found in the appendix,* drawing attention to the great increase which had taken place in the number of such recipients of relief, and suggesting that the Guardians should carry out the recommendations contained in a circular issued by the Poor Law Commissioners in 1857, viz., that all persons admitted be subjected to the provisions of the workhouse rules regarding searching, cleansing, and clothing, and also as to discipline and diet, and, especially, that no person of the class under consideration be permitted to leave the workhouse without giving three hours' previous notice. The foregoing table shows that, for the two months succeeding that in which the circular was issued, there was a decrease in the numbers so relieved as compared with the corresponding months of the previous year, but it is to be regretted that for the other months included in the table, the returns, with one exception, show an increase.

* See page 41.

10. As part of the statistics which are brought up very nearly to the date of this Report, the following table exhibits in the accustomed form:—

CLASSIFICATION of causes of Death in Workhouses, from 15th January, 1887, to 14th January, 1888.

Causes of Death.	In the four Weeks ended														Previous Year.
	12th Feb.	12th March	9th April	7th May	4th June	2nd July	30th July	27th Aug.	24th Sept.	22nd Oct.	19th Nov.	17th Dec.	14th Jan.	Total.	
Age,	231	[illegible]	[illegible]	224	161	[illegible]	148	170	181	162	214	[illegible]	270	[illegible]	[illegible]
Apoplexy,	7	7	8	7	7	1	4	4	1	8	4	6	9	[illegible]	[illegible]
Asthma,	6	8	6	6	5	8	1	8	4	7	–	8	18	37	46
Atrophy,	73	74	63	97	67	60	25	53	38	30	44	63	37	774	815
Brain Disease,	31	[illegible]	48	34	30	[illegible]	[illegible]	84	[illegible]	[illegible]	84	84	48	[illegible]	[illegible]
Cancer,	19	17	28	14	21	17	[illegible]	[illegible]	19	13	16	18	18	237	[illegible]
Childbirth,	–	–	–	7	2	–	–	3	–	–	1	1	1	10	8
Cholera,	–	–	–	–	–	–	–	–	–	–	–	–	–	–	–
Consumption,	[illegible]	95	109	103	81	[illegible]	79	61	60	64	61	81	103	[illegible]	[illegible]
Convulsions,	12	10	18	12	6	9	11	14	9	9	12	18	11	147	[illegible]
Croup,	–	8	8	5	1	–	–	–	–	–	1	1	1	16	9
Diarrhoea,	19	8	15	9	10	9	11	31	14	[illegible]	16	19	31	[illegible]	[illegible]
Dropsy,	11	10	11	14	9	10	11	16	16	17	14	16	14	154	[illegible]
Dysentery,	4	1	1	–	1	–	–	7	2	–	1	–	–	18	21
Dyspepsia,	–	2	6	2	7	8	–	3	1	3	1	1	1	[illegible]	[illegible]
Epilepsy,	7	8	4	7	8	6	10	6	9	7	8	4	8	[illegible]	41
Fever,	[illegible]	13	24	[illegible]	31	[illegible]	24	31	[illegible]	[illegible]	[illegible]	[illegible]	31	[illegible]	[illegible]
Gangrene,	8	4	7	–	3	4	4	6	4	4	1	4	4	51	47
Heart Disease,	33	41	37	45	46	[illegible]	30	30	61	33	48	45	40	497	[illegible]
Hooping-Cough,	4	6	1	1	6	3	3	6	1	17	14	4	6	73	41
Inflammation or other disease of															
Bowels,	10	6	18	9	12	4	16	18	10	11	14	9	10	137	[illegible]
Kidneys,	11	11	5	14	5	6	17	9	11	10	14	10	18	[illegible]	175
Liver,	11	10	11	10	7	6	6	6	6	4	16	11	6	112	[illegible]
Lungs,	141	175	201	153	135	[illegible]	83	71	71	79	117	161	[illegible]	1,754	[illegible]
Measles,	1	8	–	1	9	1	1	7	4	7	1	6	13	[illegible]	41
Paralysis,	77	[illegible]	80	25	[illegible]	[illegible]	19	70	15	31	29	33	33	[illegible]	[illegible]
Pleurisy,	1	1	–	–	8	1	2	1	1	8	–	6	1	[illegible]	3
Rheumatism,	5	6	6	6	12	4	1	5	7	6	6	6	4	[illegible]	[illegible]
Suicide,	1	–	7	3	3	2	1	1	–	3	1	–	2	[illegible]	[illegible]
Scrofula,	9	11	9	6	11	5	6	5	2	6	2	7	4	77	108
Small-pox,	–	–	–	–	–	–	1	1	1	–	–	–	–	3	1
Ulcers,	8	4	3	3	8	1	7	8	9	6	1	3	3	71	[illegible]
Other Diseases,	[illegible]	[illegible]	[illegible]	[illegible]	24	37	[illegible]	[illegible]	31	[illegible]	[illegible]	[illegible]	[illegible]	[illegible]	[illegible]
Total,	[illegible]	[illegible]	1,019	914	[illegible]	[illegible]	[illegible]	[illegible]	815	[illegible]	719	[illegible]	[illegible]	10,187	–
Previous year,	[illegible]	[illegible]	1,184	[illegible]	[illegible]	[illegible]	[illegible]	[illegible]	[illegible]	[illegible]	[illegible]	[illegible]	[illegible]	–	[illegible]

The total number of deaths in the workhouses in the fifty-two weeks comprised in the table has been 10,187. In the corresponding table in the last Annual Report the total number of deaths was 10,604, so that there has been a decrease of 507 deaths as compared with the number in the previous year.

Deaths by fever were 383, as against 346; by lung disease, 1,754, as against 1,848; and there were 3 deaths by small-pox, as against 1 in the previous year.

ORPHANS AND DESERTED CHILDREN.

11. The number of orphans and deserted children out at nurse from the workhouses in Ireland, under the provisions of the Act 39 and 40 Vic., c. 38, on the 29th of January last was 2,636, being an increase of 87 over the number on the corresponding date in the preceding year.

EMIGRATION.

12. In our Annual Report for 1885 we gave an account of the proceedings during the previous year under the Emigration clauses of the Arrears of Rent (Ireland) Act, 1882, and the Tramways and Public Companies (Ireland) Act, 1883.

During the year 1885 no action was taken under these clauses, but in the beginning of the year 1886 representations were made to us that there were families on the west coast of Ireland who had expressed their desire to emigrate but who had not the means to do so. We submitted the matter to His Excellency the Lord Lieutenant who authorized us to inform the Boards of Guardians of Belmullet, Clifden, Oughterard, and Westport Unions that if the Guardians effected the emigration of such persons under the provisions of the 26th section of the Irish Poor Law Amendment Act, 1849, 12 & 13 Vic., cap. 104, the sums so expended might be recouped to the Guardians from the balance of the Emigration fund under certain prescribed conditions. The Guardians of the three last mentioned Unions took no action in the matter, and the Guardians of Belmullet Union only to a very limited extent during the years 1886 and 1887. The Board of Guardians of Boyle Union applied to be allowed to participate in the offer made to the four Unions mentioned, and their application was acceded to.

Last year the following local committees who carried out emigration in previous years were re-constituted, namely, Ardfert, Cahersiveen, and Killarney, and a new committee was formed at Westport.

The following table shows the particulars respecting the persons assisted by each emigrating body:—

Union.	No. of Families.	No. of Persons.	Destination. United States.	Canada.	Australia.	Total Cost of Emigration defrayed by Government Grant. £ s. d.	Average Cost per Head. £ s. d.
Belmullet,	9	[illegible]	[illegible]	—	6	[illegible]	[illegible]
Boyle,	4	[illegible]	[illegible]	8	—	190 0 0	[illegible]
Cahersiveen, (Cahersiveen Committee)	1	6	—	—	5	[illegible]	[illegible]
Killarney, (Killarney Committee)	41	[illegible]	187	[illegible]	—	1,310 4 0	[illegible]
Tralee, (Ardfert Committee)	[illegible]	[illegible]	16	157	18	[illegible]	[illegible]
Westport, (Westport Committee)	[illegible]	116	116	—	—	1,416 13 3	[illegible]
Total,	[illegible]	[illegible]	614	[illegible]	[illegible]	[illegible]	[illegible]

The Cahercíveen Committee had submitted the names of about 1,500 persons for emigration to the United States, but owing to objections raised by the United States Government to state-aided emigrants being landed in their country, we declined to sanction their emigration. About 200 of these persons then decided to go to Canada, but they were unable to procure letters of encouragement from friends there, which was a necessary preliminary to obtaining the approval of the High Commissioner for that country.

13. We now continue the series of recent statistics by repeating, with one additional year, the table showing the number of persons assisted by Boards of Guardians to emigrate under the provisions of the Irish Poor Relief Acts, and the cost incurred for that purpose in each year, that is to say, for thirty-eight years ended on the 25th of March.

EMIGRATION under the Act 12 & 13 Vic., c. 104, sec. 26, dated 1st August, 1849.

Period.	Amount authorised to be expended by Sealed Consents.	Number of Persons assisted to Emigrate.			
		Men.	Women.	Children under 15 years of age.	Total.
	£ s. d.				
Aug., 1849, to 25 Mar., 1851,	11,151 14 11	561	1,244	787	2,592
Year ended 25 March, 1852,	21,010 5 4½	796	2,644	953	4,393
" " 1853,	14,517 0 11½	493	2,318	1,115	3,925
" " 1854,	12,146 17 6	403	1,302	896	2,601
" " 1855,	24,863 5 2½	139	2,917	738	3,794
" " 1856,	3,618 8 9	64	363	403	830
" " 1857,	2,719 13 1	76	363	363	802
" " 1858,	4,177 10 1½	38	189	302	529
" " 1859,	2,555 16 5	37	270	180	487
" " 1860,	1,729 10 2	45	178	141	364
" " 1861,	1,468 19 11	44	178	125	347
" " 1862,	528 17 4	13	72	38	123
" " 1863,	2,489 10 8	11	317	169	497
" " 1864,	4,770 4 5	123	501	345	969
" " 1865,	2,518 17 11	93	315	438	846
" " 1866,	3,423 9 11	100	380	650	1,130
" " 1867,	2,023 10 0	66	238	460	763
" " 1868,	1,983 9 6	71	263	185	519
" " 1869,	1,838 16 9	71	203	444	718
" " 1870,	1,889 12 5	49	219	449	717

EMIGRATION under the Act 12 & 13 Vic., c. 104, sec. 26, dated 1st August, 1849—*continued.*

PERIOD.	Amount authorised to be expended by Special Commissioners.	Number of Persons assisted to Emigrate.			
		Men.	Women.	Children under 15 years of age.	Total.
	£ s. d.				
Year ended 25 March, 1871,	2,269 9 11	53	226	422	701
" " 1872,	2,092 3 10	34	225	339	598
" " 1873,	1,864 14 8	44	173	364	581
" " 1874,	2,246 3 8	67	323	474	864
" " 1875,	1,917 15 1	36	199	389	624
" " 1876,	991 0 9	38	97	223	358
" " 1877,	556 17 4	13	71	116	200
" " 1878,	238 4 7	13	49	84	146
" " 1879,	551 1 9	33	82	129	244
" " 1880,	721 3 1	55	91	146	292
" " 1881,	3,482 16 0	310	558	546	1,414
" " 1882,	4,911 9 2	283	561	603	1,447
" " 1883,	4,223 16 2½	312	634	690	1,636
" " 1884,	4,340 5 2	417	840	904	2,161
" " 1885,	1,680 5 8	105	309	499	913
" " 1886,	1,153 13 1	64	233	134	431
" " 1887,	1,493 13 8	103	249	386	738
" " 1888,	1,371 0 0	116	262	342	720
Total, . . £	155,787 4 6½	5,364	12,585	16,663	41,612

AMALGAMATION OF UNIONS.

14. We have at present under consideration the question of dissolving four Unions, viz.:—Glin, Gortin, Killadysert, and Tulla, and of adding the Electoral Divisions comprised therein to the adjoining Unions. In each case we have directed an Inspector to hold the necessary preliminary inquiry and to report to us on the subject.

FINANCIAL STATISTICS OF YEAR ENDED 29TH SEPTEMBER, 1887.

15. We now proceed to the statistics arising out of the accounts of the Unions for the year ended 29th September, 1887.

We deal in the first place with Poor Relief Expenditure.

Year ended 29th September	Net Annual Value	Poor Rate lodged	Poor Relief Expenditure during the Year.						Numbers relieved.			
			In-Maintenance and Clothing.	Out-door Relief.	Cost of Relief to Blind and Deaf and Dumb [illegible]	Salaries and Rations of Officers.	All other Expenses.	Total.	In Workhouses.	Out-door.	In Blind and Deaf and Dumb Asylums.	Total.
	£	£	£	£	£	£	£	£				
[illegible]	[illegible]	[illegible]	[illegible]	[illegible]	[illegible]	[illegible]	[illegible]	[illegible]	[illegible]	[illegible]	[illegible]	[illegible]
[illegible]	[illegible]	[illegible]	[illegible]	[illegible]	[illegible]	[illegible]	[illegible]	[illegible]	[illegible]	[illegible]	[illegible]	[illegible]
Increase,	[illegible]	[illegible]	—	—	[illegible]	—	—	—	[illegible]	—	[illegible]	—
Decrease,	—	—	[illegible]	[illegible]	—	[illegible]	[illegible]	[illegible]	—	[illegible]	—	[illegible]

The fact that there has been a decrease of £12,048 in the expenditure incurred for "in-maintenance and clothing," while there has been an increase of 26,103 in the number of persons who received relief in workhouses, is mainly accounted for by the decrease in the average weekly cost per head of the persons so relieved during the year.

Treasury Subsidies.

16. The following is a statement of the Parliamentary Grant for Medical and Educational purposes, and for salaries under the "Public Health (Ireland) Act," for the year ended 25th March, 1887:—

—	Amount allowed for the Year.		
	£	s.	d.
Medical purposes, ...	73,322	5	6
Educational purposes, ...	10,313	6	6
Total for Medical and Educational purposes, .	83,635	12	0
For Salaries under Public Health Act, .	14,507	13	7
Total, ...	98,143	5	7

The total amount allowed under the Parliamentary Grant for Medical and Educational purposes for the year ended 25th March, 1887, namely, £83,635 12s. 0d., is less by £672 8s. 8d. than the amount for the previous year.

The amount for salaries under the Public Health (Ireland) Act, namely, £14,507 13s. 7d., is more by £346 4s. 11d. than the amount for the previous year.

EXPENDITURE FOR ALL PURPOSES FOR TWENTY-ONE YEARS PAST.

[illegible] Statement of the Annual Collection and Expenditure of Poor Rates for twenty-one years, ended on the [illegible] September, [illegible]; showing the Net Annual Value of property rated, the Amount of Poor Rate collected, and the Expenditure under the Poor Relief and Medical Charities Acts, &c., for each year ended [illegible] September, from [illegible] to [illegible], inclusive.

[illegible]

Hence it will be seen that while the total expenditure of Poor Rates for poor relief, medical relief, burial-grounds, sanitary measures, superannuation, payments under the Contagious Diseases (Animals) Act, payments under the National School Teachers Act, and all other purposes, was, in 1886, £1,360,597, the expenditure in 1887 was £1,338,704.

Seed Supply Act.

18. In our last Report we referred to the fact that the balance remaining unpaid of the loan obtained by Boards of Guardians in Ireland under the Seed Supply Act was due by the Guardians of forty-five Unions situated principally in the poorest parts of Ireland, and that this balance had been reduced on the 5th of February, 1887, to £42,900 1s. 11*d.* During the period from that date to the 17th of March last a sum of £7,090 12s. 10*d.* was paid to the Commissioners of Public Works, leaving a balance of £35,005 9s. 1*d.* due on the latter date by the Guardians of forty-four Unions.

The amount advanced to Boards of Guardians under the Seed Supply Act in the year 1880, after crediting the Unions with the sums refunded was £598,306 10s. 9*d.*, of which £563,301 1s. 8*d.* had been paid on the date mentioned, viz., the 17th of March last.

Markets and Fairs (Weighing of Cattle) Act, 1887.

19. On the 8th of August, 1887, "The Markets and Fairs (Weighing of Cattle) Act, 1887," became law, by which facilities were afforded for weighing cattle in markets and fairs. "Cattle" is defined by the Act to include ram, ewe, wether, lamb, and swine, and the "Market Authority" is bound to provide accommodation from the first day of the present year for weighing such cattle. Two duties devolve on our Board under this Act:—By the 6th section it is enacted that the tolls for weighing cattle should not exceed the amounts specified in the Schedule to the Act, or such other amounts as may be authorized by the Local Government Board to be taken by the market authority; and by the 9th section a market authority of any market or fair may apply to the Board to be exempted from the provisions of the Act on the ground that the sale of cattle at such market or fair is or is likely to be so small as to render it inexpedient to enforce the provision and maintenance of accommodation for weighing cattle, and the Board may thereupon declare by Order that the Act shall not apply to such market or fair until after the expiration of a time not exceeding three years.

We have not received any application to vary the scale of tolls prescribed in the schedule to the Act, but we have received 69 applications to be exempted from the provisions of the Act.

Many of the applicants rested their claims for exemption on the ground that the cost of providing weighing accommodation would far exceed the tolls received in a year, and, further, that the accommodation when so provided would not be used; we could not, however, entertain such considerations, as the Act empowers us to make the exemption solely on the ground of the smallness of the sales. We acceded to 7 applications, having previously by public advertisements invited objections, and an Order of exemption was made for one year in each case.

MEDICAL CHARITIES ACT, AND VACCINATION ACTS.

20. We next submit to your Excellency a report of the proceedings under these Acts for the year ended 30th September, 1887.

The annexed table exhibits, in the usual form, the fluctuations in the number of cases in which medical relief was afforded under the Medical Charities Act, during each of the twelve years ended 30th September, 1887, in each province, and for the whole of Ireland.

In Ulster there has been an increase of 3,417 in the number of cases prescribed for at the dispensaries, and a decrease of 720 in the number of those attended at their own houses.

In Munster there has been a decrease of 899 in the number of cases prescribed for at the dispensaries, and a decrease of 3,201 in the number of those attended at their own houses.

In Leinster there has been an increase of 6,085 in the number of cases prescribed for at the dispensaries, and an increase of 2,560 in the number of those attended at their own houses.

In Connaught there has been a decrease of 2,571 in the number of cases prescribed for at the dispensaries, and a decrease of 2,241 in the number of those attended at their own houses.

The last three columns in the table show an increase of 2,039 cases for all Ireland, including both classes, as compared with the previous year.

[TABLE

C

Vaccination.

21. In the following table is shown the number of cases of vaccination by Medical Officers of Dispensary Districts in each year from 1855 to 1887, the Compulsory Vaccination Act having been passed in 1863:—

TABLE.

—	Number of Cases of Vaccination.	—	Number of Cases of Vaccination.
Year ended Sept. 30th, 1855,	46,711	Year ended Sept. 30th, 1872,	262,484
" " 1856,	64,131	" " 1873,	136,873
" " 1857,	47,855	" " 1874,	132,567
" " 1858,	54,984	" " 1875,	137,340
" " 1859,	140,411	" " 1876,	114,482
" " 1860,	107,305	" " 1877,	117,079
" " 1861,	90,256	" " 1878,	133,045
" " 1862,	69,668	" " 1879,	126,911
" " 1863,	106,310	" " 1880,	147,869
" " 1864,	191,610	" " 1881,	113,557
" " 1865,	169,142	" " 1882,	108,575
" " 1866,	137,124	" " 1883,	106,071
" " 1867,	125,741	" " 1884,	102,546
" " 1868,	131,426	" " 1885,	102,619
" " 1869,	125,672	" " 1886,	94,861
" " 1870,	140,220	" " 1887,	96,499
" " 1871,	178,889		

The following table contains a summary of the total number of cases of vaccination during the year ended 30th September 1887, the cases being classified under the headings, "under one year old when vaccinated," "above one year old when vaccinated," and "other persons."

—	Children born since 1st January, 1864.		Other Persons.	Total.
	Under one year old when Vaccinated.	Above one year old when Vaccinated.		
Total of Ireland, . .	80,789	12,160	3,550	96,499

Vaccine Department.

22. During the year ended 31st of March, 1888, 3,726 applications were received from Medical Officers of workhouses and dispensaries and other public institutions, from Military Medical Officers stationed in Ireland, and from private practitioners, for lymph; and 19,601 points, and 2,310 tubes charged with lymph were distributed. During the same period 1,826 vaccinations were performed at the stations in Sackville-street, and York-street, Dublin.

SMALL-POX.

23. The number of deaths in workhouses from small-pox and the number of cases of the disease treated by Dispensary Medical Officers in each of the last twenty-four years are given in the following table:—

DEATHS in WORKHOUSES from SMALL-POX, and NUMBER of CASES of SMALL-POX treated by DISPENSARY MEDICAL OFFICERS.

Deaths in Workhouses from Small-pox.		Number of Cases of Small-pox treated by Medical Officers of Dispensary Districts.	
PERIOD. 52 Weeks ended	Number of Deaths.	PERIOD. Year ended	Number of Cases.
11th February, 1865, . .	145	30th September, 1864, . .	1,963
10th February, 1866, . .	59	30th September, 1865, . .	2,080
9th February, 1867, . .	9	30th September, 1866, . .	876
8th February, 1868, . .	5	30th September, 1867, . .	165
6th February, 1869, . .	8	30th September, 1868, . .	455
5th February, 1870, . .	1	30th September, 1869, . .	27
4th February, 1871, . .	13	30th September, 1870, . .	51
3rd February, 1872, . .	462	30th September, 1871, . .	773
1st February, 1873, . .	677	30th September, 1872, . .	10,317
31st January, 1874, . .	110	30th September, 1873, . .	859
30th January, 1875, . .	142	30th September, 1874, . .	961
29th January, 1876, . .	41	30th September, 1875, . .	231
27th January, 1877, . .	2	30th September, 1876, . .	29
26th January, 1878, . .	12	30th September, 1877, . .	117
25th January, 1879, . .	234	30th September, 1878, . .	1,239
24th January, 1880, . .	113	30th September, 1879, . .	1,311
22nd January, 1881, . .	67	30th September, 1880, . .	863
21st January, 1882, . .	64	30th September, 1881, . .	114
20th January, 1883, . .	76	30th September, 1882, . .	479
19th January, 1884, . .	11	30th September, 1883, . .	91
17th January, 1885, . .	1	30th September, 1884, . .	18
16th January, 1886, . .	2	30th September, 1885, . .	17
15th January, 1887, . .	1	30th September, 1886, . .	11
14th January, 1888, . .	6	30th September, 1887, . .	18

The following table shows in each province the quarters of the year when the disease most prevailed:—

SUMMARY of SMALL-POX cases attended by Dispensary Medical Officers during the year ended 30th September, 1887,—taken from their quarterly Returns.

PROVINCES.	Quarter, 31st Dec., 1886.	Quarter, 31st Mar., 1887.	Quarter, 30th June, 1887.	Quarter, 30th Sept., 1887.	Total.
Ulster, . . .	1	-	5	5	11
Munster, . . .	1	1	1	2	5
Leinster, . . .	-	-	1	1	2
Connaught, . . .	-	-	-	-	-
Total Ireland, .	2	1	7	8	18

Fever in Dispensary Districts.

24. The following is a return of the number of cases of fever reported as attended by the Medical Officers of Dispensary Districts during each of the twenty-three years ended 30th September, 1887, beginning with 26,566 cases in 1865, and ending with 5,092 in 1887:—

Year ended 30th September.	Number of Cases.	Decrease per Year.	Increase.
1865,	26,566	-	-
1866,	22,287	4,279	-
1867,	18,975	3,312	-
1868,	17,400	1,575	-
1869,	16,882	518	-
1870,	15,744	1,138	-
1871,	15,574	170	-
1872,	15,594	-	20
1873,	14,434	1,160	-
1874,	14,424	10	-
1875,	13,280	1,144	-
1876,	11,646	1,634	-
1877,	11,396	250	-
1878,	10,945	451	-
1879,	10,989	-	44
1880,	11,201	-	212
1881,	9,713	1,488	-
1882,	8,329	1,384	-
1883,	8,051	278	-
1884,	6,400	1,651	-
1885,	5,768	632	-
1886,	5,045	723	-
1887,	5,092	-	47

There were 3,819 cases of scarlatina treated by Medical Officers of Dispensary Districts in 1887, as compared with 2,702 cases in 1886, being an increase of 1,117.

25. The next table gives the expenditure under the Medical Charities and Vaccination Acts for the last twelve years, ended 29th September, 1887.

[Table.

MEDICAL CHARITIES EXPENDITURE, Year ended 29th September.

Year.	Ulster.	Munster.	Leinster.	Connaught.	Total.
	£	£	£	£	£
1876, .	40,083	38,604	42,828	19,009	141,463
1877, .	39,368	39,663	43,348	18,703	141,076
1878, .	39,561	42,274	44,030	19,074	144,913
1879, .	40,263	40,637	44,880	20,230	146,030
1880, .	43,948	43,168	45,808	21,114	153,875
1881, .	43,640	44,065	47,429	22,110	157,244
1882, .	44,639	44,688	47,869	21,967	159,028
1883, .	43,814	45,098	48,678	22,170	159,405
1884, .	42,838	44,768	48,805	22,387	158,363
1885, .	41,776	46,331	48,184	24,434	160,467
1886, .	42,064	44,016	49,809	23,021	158,112
1887, .	42,253	44,276	49,681	22,164	158,376

And the following shows in more detail, and under the usual heads, a comparative statement of the expenditure for the two years ended September 29th, 1886 and 1887, respectively:—

MEDICAL CHARITIES EXPENDITURE.

—	1886.	1887.
	£	£
1. Medicines and medical appliances, ...	26,847	26,465
2. Rent of Dispensary buildings, ...	8,424	8,348
3. Books, forms, stationery, printing, and advertising.	909	1,187
4. Salaries of { Medical Officers, ...	60,372	60,107
{ Apothecaries, ...	2,815	2,629
5. Fuel, porters, and incidental expenses, . . .	19,043	20,189
EXPENSES UNDER VACCINATION ACTS:		
6. Vaccination fees and other expenses:—		
Fees to Medical Officers, ...	9,842	9,066
Other expenses, ...	1,970	1,827
Total, ...	158,113	158,570

Dispensary Houses and Dwelling-Houses for Medical Officers.

26. In paragraph 24 of our last Report we referred to the proceedings under the "Act to give facilities for providing Dispensary houses and Dwelling-houses for Medical Officers of Dispensary Districts in certain parts of Ireland."

Advantage still continues to be taken of the provisions of the Act, and certificates have been issued since our last Report in the following cases:—

—	Dispensary District.	Union.
Dispensary and Dispensary Residence,	*Foxford,	Swinford.
Do., do.,	*Rathcoole,	Celbridge.
Do., do.,	*Millstreet,	Millstreet.
Dispensary Residence,	Tubbercurry,	Tobercurry.
Dispensary and Dispensary Residence,	*Rathvilly,	Baltinglass.
Do., do.,	Clara,	Tullamore.
Two Dispensaries,	North City,	Dublin, North.
Dispensary and Dispensary Residence,	Lettermore,	Oughterard.
Dispensary Residence,	[illegible],	Carrickmacross.
Dispensary and Dispensary Residence,	Clarina,	Limerick.
Dispensary,	Enniskillen,	Enniskillen.
Dispensary and Dispensary Residence,	Benburb,	Dungannon.
Dispensary Residence,	Dromahaire,	Manorhamilton.
Dispensary and Dispensary Residence,	*Ballindine,	Claremorris.
Do., do.,	Lurgan,	Lurgan.

* The certificates in these cases were supplemental to other certificates granted for loans which were found to be insufficient for the purposes required.

SANITARY ACTS.

Provisional Orders.

27. Since our last Report we have issued the following Provisional Orders:—

Date.	Place.	Purpose.
2nd May, 1887,	Town of Wexford,	Directing the Grand Jury of the County of Wexford to contribute a sum of [illegible] a year to the maintenance of the Mail Car Roads within the Borough of Wexford.
6th May, 1887,	City of Dublin,	Empowering the Corporation of the City of Dublin, the Urban Sanitary Authority, to put in force the provisions of the Lands Clauses Acts with reference to the purchase and taking of lands, otherwise than by agreement, in regard to certain lands required for the purpose of making a new street from Mullinahack, New Row West, to Usher's-quay.

Provisional Orders—continued.

Date.	Place.	Purpose.
6th May, 1887,	Strabane Union, .	Empowering the Board of Guardians of Strabane Union, the Rural Sanitary Authority, to put in force the provisions of the Lands Clauses Acts respecting the purchase and taking of lands, otherwise than by agreement, with reference to certain lands required for the purpose of providing a supply of water for the town of Strabane.
18th May, 1887,	Belfast Union, .	Empowering the Board of Guardians of Belfast Union, the Rural Sanitary Authority, to put in force the provisions of the Lands Clauses Acts with reference to the purchase and taking of lands, otherwise than by agreement, in regard to certain lands and premises required for the purpose of providing a supply of water for the villages of Greencastle and Upper Whitehouse.
20th May, 1887,	Ballyshannon Union,	Empowering the Board of Guardians of Ballyshannon Union, the Rural Sanitary Authority, to put in force the provisions of the Lands Clauses Acts respecting the purchase and taking of lands, otherwise than by agreement, with reference to certain lands required for the purpose of providing a supply of water for the town of Ballyshannon.
30th May, 1887,	Ballyshannon Union,	Empowering the Board of Guardians of Ballyshannon Union, the Rural Sanitary Authority, to put in force the provisions of the Lands Clauses Acts with reference to the purchase and taking of lands, otherwise than by agreement, in regard to certain lands required for the purpose of providing a supply of water for the village of Kinlough.
26th May, 1887,	Killiney and Ballybrack Township.	Separating the Township of Killiney and Ballybrack from the Rathdown Union Rural Sanitary District, and constituting it an Urban Sanitary District.
7th July, 1887,	Bangor Town, . .	Separating the Town of Bangor from the Newtownards Union Rural Sanitary District, and constituting it an Urban Sanitary District.
24th Jan., 1888,	Warrenpoint Town, .	Vesting the Warrenpoint Waterworks in the Warrenpoint Urban Sanitary Authority, and adjusting the accounts between the said Urban Authority and the Newry Union Rural Sanitary Authority.
16th Mar., 1888,	Tanderagee Town, .	Separating the Town of Tanderagee from the Banbridge Union Rural Sanitary District, and constituting it an Urban Sanitary District.
28th Mar., 1888,	Coleraine Town, .	Separating a certain area recently added to the town of Coleraine under the Towns Improvement (Ireland) Act, 1854, from the Coleraine Union Rural Sanitary District, and including it in the Coleraine Urban Sanitary District.
31st Mar., 1888,	Longford Union, .	Empowering the Board of Guardians of Longford Union, the Rural Sanitary Authority, to put in force the provisions of the Lands Clauses Acts with reference to the purchase and taking of Lands, otherwise than by agreement, in regard to certain lands and premises required for the purpose of providing a supply of water for the town of Longford.

Provisional Orders—continued.

We have received petitions for Provisional Orders in the following cases, and the petitions are under consideration.

Place.	Purpose.
Dublin City, . . .	To put in force the provisions of the Lands Clauses Acts with reference to the purchase and taking of lands, otherwise than by agreement, required for the purpose of providing a market-place for the sale of vegetables and fish.
Lismore Union, . .	To put in force the provisions of the Lands Clauses Acts with reference to the purchase and taking of lands, otherwise than by agreement, required for the purpose of providing a Water Supply for the Town of Cappoquin.
Tuam Union, .	To put in force the provisions of the Lands Clauses Acts with reference to the purchase and taking of lands, otherwise than by agreement, required for the purpose of providing a Water Supply for the Town of Tuam.
Lurgan Town, . .	To put in force the provisions of the Lands Clauses Acts with reference to the purchase and taking of lands, otherwise than by agreement, required for market purposes.
Ballymoney Town, .	To constitute the Town of Ballymoney an Urban Sanitary District.
Kilrush Town, . .	To adjust the accounts between the Kilrush Urban and Rural Sanitary Authorities in pursuance of the 277th Section of the Public Health (Ireland) Act, 1878.
Clones Town, . .	To constitute the Town of Clones an Urban Sanitary District.

Towns Improvement (Ireland) Act, 1854.

26. We have given our consent to the extension of the boundaries of the town of Coleraine in pursuance of section 5 of the above-mentioned Act.

Applications were made by certain of the inhabitants of the towns of Bantry, of Downpatrick, and of Passage West and Monkstown to have the provisions of the Act carried into effect in these places. In Bantry and in Downpatrick the ratepayers at the meetings convened to consider the question decided not to adopt the provisions of the Act, and in the case of Passage West and Monkstown the arrangements preliminary to holding the requisite meeting have not been completed.

29. The following is a list of By-laws submitted to and confirmed by us during the year 1887–8 :—

Place.	Subject.
Killiney and Ballybrack Township,	Bathing.
Bray Township,	New Streets. New Buildings, &c. Closing of Buildings unfit for human habitation. Cleansing of Footways and Premises, &c. Keeping of Animals. Common Lodging-houses. Houses let in Lodgings other than Common Lodging-houses. Slaughter-houses. Regulation of Markets.
Warrenpoint Town,	Regulation of Markets.
Clonmel Town,	Cleansing of Footways and Premises. Nuisances. Common Lodging-houses. Houses let in Lodgings other than Common Lodging-houses. New Buildings. Slaughter-houses.
	Tolls.
Bray Township,	Market Tolls approved.
Warrenpoint Town,	Market Tolls approved.

30. Consent has been given to the alteration of the days for holding Fairs in the Town of Clonakilty. We have under consideration a similar application in regard to the Fairs held in the Town of Swinsford.

Burial Grounds.

31. Orders have been made and gazetted prohibiting further interments in the burial grounds named hereunder :—

1. St. Michael's Burial Ground, in the City of Limerick.
2. The burial ground situate at Templeshannon, in the Poor Law Union of Enniscorthy.

Of these Orders one was made subject to certain exceptions mentioned therein, and we retain power to grant licences for burial in certain cases, from time to time, if it should appear to us expedient to do so.

Public Health.

32. Our report upon Public Health is continued from the last Annual Report. Details were given therein of the operations in regard to sewerage and water-supply under the provisions of the Public Health Act, 1878, in continuation of the detail of pro-

ceedings under the Act of 1874; the extent of those operations is still in some degree measured in Rural Sanitary Districts by the number of the Orders under seal fixing the area of charge for each such operation, and the loans borrowed for those purposes through the Public Works Commissioners.

In the year 1875-76 the number of such Orders was 70; in 1876-77 it was 89; in 1877-78 it was 122; in 1878-79 it was 117; in 1879-80 it was 126; in 1880-81 it was 103; in 1881-82 it was 79; in 1882-83 it was 83; in 1883-84 it was 79; in 1884-85 it was 102; in 1885-86 it was 87, and in 1886-87 it was 74. From 26th March, 1887, to the 25th March, 1888, the number of additional Orders has been 60, issued to 51 different Unions.

On the whole, therefore, 1,220 Orders fixing areas of charge for sewerage or water-supply, or both, have been issued during the last thirteen years.

The preceding statements relate to Rural Sanitary Districts. In Urban Districts all sanitary expenses are chargeable upon funds levied from the whole district.

Loans.

83. In both Urban and Rural Sanitary Districts a considerable part of the expenditure on sewerage, water-supply, and other local improvements is carried out by means of loans which, on our recommendation, are issued to the Sanitary Authority in each case by the Public Works Commissioners.

In the twelve years ended 31st March, 1887, loans were recommended as follows:—

Year ended		Amount. £	s.	d.
31st March, 1876,	.	37,584	0	0
„ 1877,	.	41,085	0	0
„ 1878,	.	82,056	0	0
„ 1879,	.	124,454	0	0
„ 1880,	.	292,824	0	0
„ 1881,	.	199,259	0	0
„ 1882,	.	202,374	0	0
„ 1883,	.	86,954	0	0
„ 1884,	.	179,838	0	0
„ 1885,	.	161,599	0	0
„ 1886,	.	170,161	9	9
„ 1887,	.	83,224	7	8
Total, .	.	1,680,393	17	5

The following is a list of loans sanctioned by us during the year ended the 31st March, 1888, in continuation of similar lists in previous Reports.

LIST of LOANS sanctioned during the year ended the 31st March, 1888, in continuation of similar lists in previous Reports.

Name of Sanitary District.		Amount of Loan.	Purpose for which obtained.	Date of Sanction.
		£ s. d.		
Antrim,	Rural,	80 0 0	Antrim Sewerage.	8th June, 1887.
Athlone,	do., .	800 0 0	Carraghboy Well and Pump.	14th October, 1887.
Ballina,	do., .	150 0 0	Erecting Gatekeeper's Lodge at Leigue Cemetery.	20th February, 1888.
Ballinasloe,	do., .	105 0 0	Kiltormer Pump.	1st November, 1887.
Ballyshannon,	do., .	6,000 0 0	Ballyshannon Water Supply.	17th February, 1888.
Do.,	do., .	500 0 0	Kinlough Water Supply.	20th February, 1888.
Belfast,	do., .	600 0 0	Greencastle and Upper Whitehouse Sewerage.	9th April, 1887.
Carrick-on-Suir,	Urban, .	600 0 0	Widening and Improving Streets.	18th February, 1888.
Cashel	do., .	83 0 0	Erecting Caretaker's House at Waterworks.	3rd August, 1887.
Cork,	do., .	1,000 0 0	Erecting Houses under the Labouring Classes Lodging Houses Acts.	24th August, 1887.
Corrofin, Rural,	.	50 0 0	Erecting Pump at Corrofin.	16th May, 1887.
Dalkey,	Urban, .	250 0 0	Constructing New Street in continuation of Vico Road.	9th September, 1887.
Do.,	do., .	283 0 0	Sewerage, Sorrento Terrace and part of Vico Road.	27th September, 1887.
Do.,	do., .	180 0 0	Main Sewer, Sorrento Road.	1st November, 1887.
Dublin, North,	Rural,	285 0 0	New Sewer, North Circular Road.	29th November, 1887.
Dublin,	Urban,	7,200 0 0	Purchase of Property required for the formation of a New Street from Mullinahack to Usher's-quay.	15th March, 1888.
Galway,	do., .	3,000 0 0	Construction of Claddagh Bridge.	23rd April, 1887.
Do.,	do., .	680 0 0	Purchase and re-modelling of Houses under the Labouring Classes Lodging Houses Acts.	1st September, 1887.
Do.,	do., .	25 0 0	Do. (Additional Loan).	13th February, 1888.
Glin,	Rural, .	100 0 0	Constructing Filter Beds and Reservoir at Shanagolden.	25th August, 1887.
Do.,	do., .	216 0 0	Glin Water Supply.	2nd December, 1887.
Inishowen,	do., .	800 0 0	Buncrana Waterworks Extension.	5th November, 1887.
Kilkenny,	Urban, .	7,000 0 0	Erecting Houses under the Labouring Classes Lodging Houses Acts.	2nd June, 1887.

List of Loans sanctioned during the year ended the 31st March, 1888, in continuation of similar lists in previous Reports—*continued.*

Name of Sanitary District.		Amount of Loan.			Purposes for which obtained.	Date of Sanction.
		£	s.	d.		
Killarney,	Rural, .	600	0	0	Killorglin Sewerage, .	17th May, 1887.
Kilrush,	do., .	300	0	0	Improvement of Burial Ground at Shanakyle.	1st April, 1887.
Kingstown,	Urban, .	100	0	0	Purchase of Horses, &c., for scavenging purposes.	7th September, 1887.
Kinsale,	do., .	1,800	0	0	Erecting Houses under the Labouring Classes Lodging Houses Acts.	16th September, 1887.
Do.,	do., .	1,000	0	0	Do., do.	20th December, 1887.
Larne,	Rural, .	150	0	0	Glenarm Water Supply,	11th February, 1888.
Limerick,	Urban, .	3,710	0	0	Sewerage, . . .	12th January, 1888.
Londonderry,	do., .	4,500	0	0	Waterside Water Works,	9th August, 1887.
Macroom,	Rural, .	55	0	0	Macroom Sewerage (additional loan).	21st September, 1887.
Mallow,	do., .	150	0	0	Erecting Caretaker's Lodge at Mallow Cemetery.	29th July, 1887.
Mount Bellew, do.,	.	140	0	0	Castleblakeney Water Supply.	2nd April, 1887.
Mullingar,	do., .	2,000	0	0	Expenses of obtaining Mullingar Water Act	11th May, 1887.
Omagh,	Rural, .	600	0	0	Additional Water Supply at Omagh.	15th April, 1887.
Rathmines and Rathgar,	Urban.	30,000	0	0	Water Works (additional loan).	14th October, 1887.
Sligo,	Rural, .	100	0	0	Erecting Pump at Cliffoney.	31st July, 1887.
Strabane,	do., .	2,500	0	0	Strabane Water Supply.	27th September, 1887.
Trim,	Urban, .	1,600	0	0	Erecting Houses under the Labouring Classes Lodging Houses Acts.	8th June, 1887.
Warrenpoint,	do., .	100	0	0	To complete Town Hall,	18th October, 1887.
Waterford,	Rural, .	618	10	6	Tramore Sewerage, .	„ „
Wexford,	Urban, .	2,500	0	0	Erecting Houses under the Labouring Classes Lodging Houses Acts.	9th January, 1888.
Wicklow,	do., .	289	16	1	Sanitary Works, . .	6th January, 1888.
Youghal,	do., .	400	0	0	Erecting Market-house,	12th May, 1887.

The total amount of the loans included in the above list is £83,003 8s 0d., which, added to the previous sums, constitutes a total of £1,714,297 6s. 2d. for the thirteen years in question.

This expenditure, which is independent of disbursements from the current rates for the same purposes, relates mainly to the cost of structural works for water-supply and sewerage.

Labourers Acts.

34. The following Table shows the Unions from which petitions for confirmation of Improvement Schemes were received by us from the inception of these Acts up to the 31st March, 1888, the number of houses applied for in each case, the number actually authorized up to that date, and the number included in applications which remain to be disposed of. The amounts of the loans sanctioned by the Treasury for the purposes of the Acts are also given.

Table.

Union.	Number of Cottages applied for.	Number of Cottages authorized.	Number of Cottages included in applications which are still pending.	Total amount of Loans sanctioned by the Treasury. £	s.	d.
Abbeyleix,	90	25	-	-		
Ardee,	191	188	-	15,618	10	0
Athy,	301	128	-	12,041	0	0
Bailieborough,	48	15	-	-		
Ballinasloe,	14	5	-	1,160	0	0
Ballymahon,	171	57	-	4,500	0	0
Ballymena,	34	16	-	1,900	0	0
Ballyshannon,	29	-	-	-		
Balrothery,	85	59	-	6,150	0	0
Baltinglass,	129	60	3	6,100	0	0
Bandon,	220	188	-	15,000	0	0
Borrisokane,	78	41	-	8,400	0	0
Callan,	58	35	-	2,600	0	0
Carlow,	231	144	-	9,626	0	0
Carrickmacross,	45	-	-	-		
Carrick-on-Shannon,	15	5	-	375	0	0
Carrick-on-Suir,	71	46	-	6,770	0	0
Cashel,	330	208	73	13,700	0	0
Castlecomer,	47	23	-	2,163	0	0
Cavan,	107	-	72	-		
Celbridge,	94	87	-	-		
Clogheen,	197	56	139	3,000	0	0
Clonakilty,	179	128	-	12,050	0	0
Clonmel,	93	46	-	1,820	0	0
Cork,	438	257	-	26,000	0	0
Corrofin,	18	9	-	1,015	10	0
Croom,	256	187	-	18,4[illegible]5	0	0
Delvin,	379	185	-	22,240	0	0
Dingle,	20	-	20	-		
Drogheda,	603	514	-	40,970	0	0
Dromore, West,	71	7	-	630	0	0
Dublin, North,	70	60	-	4,710	0	0
Dublin, South	38	26	-	-		
Dundalk,	109	43	-	900	0	0
Dungarvan,	68	47	-	4,979	0	0
Dunmanway,	304	187	-	18,770	0	0
Dunshaughlin,	184	75	-	9,030	0	0
Edenderry,	40	-	40	-		
Ennis,	177	109	-	1,824	0	7

TABLE—*continued.*

Union.	Number of Cottages applied for.	Number of Cottages authorized.	Number of Cottages included in special schemes which are still pending.	Total amount of Loans sanctioned by the Treasury.		
				£	s.	d.
Enniscorthy,	198	88	117	8,280	0	0
Ennistymon,	104	87	–	–		
Fermoy,	258	147	–	1,758	9	0
Glin,	180	60	100	6,150	0	0
Gorey,	185	90	–	8,895	0	0
Gort,	30	5	–	–		
Granard,	103	96	–	9,600	0	0
Kanturk,	403	820	–	82,600	0	0
Kells,	301	183	–	12,000	0	0
Kilkenny,	78	34	–	–		
Killadysert,	119	18	91	1,855	0	0
Killarney,	286	131	–	–		
Kilmacthomas,	259	129	–	11,109	0	0
Kilmallock,	1,184	364	477	81,575	0	0
Kilrush,	78	31	–	–		
Kinsale,	102	42	–	4,680	0	0
Limerick,	1,244	893	217	37,010	0	0
Lismore,	252	184	–	7,000	0	0
Listowel,	170	110	–	10,900	0	0
Longford,	70	46	–	0,880	0	0
Loughrea,	43	10	–	–		
Macroom,	697	318	277	30,580	0	0
Mallow,	201	111	–	2,783	0	0
Manorhamilton,	42	17	–	1,060	10	0
Midleton,	303	300	–	25,070	0	0
Millstreet,	125	108	–	10,800	0	0
Mitchelstown,	216	107	69	8,900	0	0
Mohill,	48	17	–	1,700	0	0
Mountmellick,	262	91	171	1,610	0	0
Mullingar,	804	203	–	20,797	10	4
Naas,	239	100	–	7,044	0	0
Navan,	318	318	–	28,140	0	0
Nenagh,	333	209	–	30,878	17	4
Newcastle,	850	270	–	26,700	0	0
New Ross,	302	84	210	2,308	13	8
Oldcastle,	240	188	–	21,560	0	0
Parsonstown,	75	46	–	4,570	0	0
Rathdrum,	36	19	–	1,430	0	0
Rathkeale,	831	107	116	11,807	0	0
Roscommon,	7	–	7	–		
Scariff,	77	35	–	8,013	0	0
Shillelagh,	20	18		2,143	0	0
Skibbereen,	347	113	110	12,045	0	0
Skull,	47	13	–	1,235	0	0
Sligo,	19	–	–	–		
Strokestown,	81	–	–	–		
Thomastown,	73	42	31	8,367	0	0
Thurles,	107	38	56	–		
Tipperary,	677	370	–	42,010	0	0
Tralee,	420	180	100	18,812	0	0
Trim,	204	92	98	0,508	10	0
Tulla,	276	134	–	6,003	3	0
Tullamore,	257	83	111	8,580	0	0
Urlingford,	78	–	78	–		
Waterford,	138	107	–	8,000	0	0
Wexford,	383	323	–	27,157	0	0
Youghal,	351	215	–	8,010	0	0
Total,	10,600	8,553	2,010	£830,007	14	0

Following the course adopted in previous Reports, we now give tables showing what has been done by Sanitary Authorities under the Improvement Schemes authorized, and what is proposed to be done under further Improvement Schemes.

Table I shows that out of the 9,552 houses authorized, 3,172 have been built, and 2,776 of these actually let, and that 1,792 others are at present in progress of erection.

Table II. shows that further Improvement Schemes have been, or are, we understand, about to be, submitted to us, embracing 3,731 cottages at an estimated cost of about £395,437.

TABLE I.—RETURN showing what has been done under Improvement Schemes Authorized.

UNIONS.	No. of Electoral Divisions in which the erection of houses has been authorized.	Number of Houses						
		Authorized.	Built.	In progress.	Not yet commenced.	Abandoned.	Actually Let.	Rent (*Weekly*).
PROVINCE OF ULSTER.								
CO. ANTRIM.								
Ballymena, ...	6	18	.	.	18	.	.	—
CO. CAVAN.								
Bailieborough, . . .	5	15	.	.	15	.	.	—
Total for Ulster, . .	11	33	.	.	33	.	.	—
PROVINCE OF MUNSTER.								
CO. CLARE.								
Corofin, ...	6	9	.	9	.	.	.	1s. and 1s. 2d.
Ennis, ...	17	103	15	7	81	.	11	1s. 3d.
Ennistymon, . . .	13	27	.	.	27	.	.	—
Kildysart, . . .	9	19	11	1	.	7	10	10d. and 11d.
Kilrush, ...	17	31	.	.	31	.	.	—
Scariff, ...	14	26	.	.	26	.	.	—
Tulla, ...	17	134	68	.	46	20	67	9d.
CO. CORK.								
Bandon, ...	19	127 & 11 to be repaired.	.	27	93 & 11 to be repaired.	7	.	—
Clonakilty, . . .	18	131	9	90	31	1	8	1s.
Cork, ...	26	265 & 1 to be repaired.	14	73	172 & 1 to be repaired.	6	10	1s.
Dunmanway, . . .	18	187	77	98	12	.	.	—
Fermoy, ...	21	162	18	.	144	.	18	1s.
Kanturk, ...	23	320	184	134	2	.	160	10d.
Kinsale, ...	13	41	.	.	41	.	.	—
Macroom, ...	26	318	67	112	129	10	67	1s. and 10d.
Mallow, ...	19	110 & 1 to be repaired.	76	8	26 & 1 to be repaired.	.	24	1s.

TABLE I.—RETURN showing what has been done under Improvement Schemes Authorized—*continued.*

Unions.	No. of Electoral Divisions in which the erection of houses has been sanctioned.	Number of Houses						
		Authorized.	Built.	In progress.	Not yet commenced.	Abandoned.	Actually Let.	Rent (Weekly).
PROVINCE OF MUNSTER—*continued.*								
Co. CORK—*continued.*								
Midleton,	10	200 (including 1 conditionally).	.	.	200 (including 1 conditionally).	.	.	—
Millstreet,	11	108	.	108	.	.	.	6d.
Mitchelstown,	16	107	30	.	14	19	10	1s.
Skibbereen,	20	109 & 3 to be repaired.	.	107 & 3 repairing.	.	2	.	—
Skull,	6	18	.	.	18	.	.	—
Youghal,	14	218	37	7	173	1	29	1s. and 1d.
Co. KERRY.								
Killarney,	27	131	.	.	126	5	.	—
Listowel,	31	110	.	12	91	7	.	—
Tralee,	26	300	198	.	.	92	198	average 9d.
Co. LIMERICK.								
Croom,	20	131 and 2 to be repaired.	13	81 and 2 repairing.	37	7	43	11½d.
Glin,	13	66	60	.	.	6	60	10d.
Kilmallock,	20	324	240	44	.	76	240	10½d. and 1s.
Limerick,	23	291	131	99	43	61	149	average 9d.
Newcastle,	31	263 and 3 to be repaired.	130	100 and 3 repairing.	60	6	109	average 10d.
Rathkeale,	18	167	18	85	.	9	43	9d. and 1s.
Co. TIPPERARY.								
Borrisokane,	8	41	1	8	33	7	1	1s.
Carrick-on-Suir,	17	49 and 1 to be repaired.	6	16	17 and 1 to be repaired.	10	6	1s.
Cashel,	24	208	108	35	24	45	109	10d. and 1s. 1d.
Clogheen,	9	26	14	.	.	3	14	1s.
Clonmel,	7	83 and 4 to be repaired.	11	.	67 and 4 to be repaired.	6	11	1s.
Nenagh,	27	269	118	89	171	1	62	10d., 11d. and 1s. 3d.
Thurles,	16	35	.	.	34	.	.	—
Tipperary,	28	276	146	119	41	21	145	1s.
Co. WATERFORD.								
Dungarvan,	13	47	6	23	19	.	6	1s. 6d.
Kilmacthomas,	14	123	91	18	14	8	71	9½d.
Lismore,	14	124	80	4	43	1	45	11d.
Waterford,	26	167	48	6	109	4	40	1s.
Total for Munster,	745	4,02[illegible] and 99 to be repaired.	2,714	1,28[illegible] and 11 repairing.	1,22[illegible] and 14 to be repaired.	416	1,038	—

TABLE I.—RETURN showing what has been done under Improvement Schemes Authorized—*continued.*

UNIONS.	No. of Electoral Divisions in which the erection of houses has been authorized.	Number of Houses						
		Authorized.	Built.	In progress.	Not yet commenced.	Abandoned.	Actually Let.	Rent (Weekly.)
PROVINCE OF LEINSTER.								
CO. CARLOW.								
Carlow,	23	143 and 9 to be repaired.	31	8	103 and 9 to be repaired.	.	28	1s.
CO. DUBLIN.								
Balrothery,	10	63	41	6	8	8	37	1s. and 1s. 6d.
Dublin, North,	6	60	36	16	10	.	33	1s. 6d.
„ South,	8	78	.	.	78	.	.	—
CO. KILDARE.								
Athy,	38	118 and 9 to be repaired.	45 and 9 repaired.	29	58	13	29	1s.
Celbridge,	18	37	.	.	37	.	.	—
Naas,	23	104 and 8 to be repaired.	17	28	43 and 8 to be repaired.	.	17 and 20 others practically let.	1s.
CO. KILKENNY.								
Callan,	16	35	.	26	8	6	.	—
Castlecomer,	6	23	.	.	22	.	.	—
Kilkenny,	18	34	.	.	63	1	.	—
Thomastown,	16	40	10	6	23	.	17	average, 9d.
KING'S CO.								
Parsonstown,	11	43 and 4 to be repaired.	.	14	23 and 4 to be repaired.	2	.	—
Tullamore,	18	83	63	12	8	8	43	1s.
CO. LONGFORD.								
Ballymahon,	18	87	31	14	42	1	28	9d.
Granard,	26	98	.	.	98	.	.	—
Longford,	10	45	5	20	18	.	8	1s. 2d.
CO. LOUTH.								
Ardee,	13	132 and 8 to be repaired.	.	10	118 and 3 to be repaired.	3	.	—
Drogheda,	12	288 and 4 to be repaired.	87	34	191 and 8 to be repaired.	1	85	1s.
Dundalk,	7	63	6	.	57	.	6	1s.
CO. MEATH.								
Dunshaughlin,	19	78	17	9	51	6	13	10d.
Kells,	23	193	68	21	136	14	48	1s. 1d.
Navan,	13	218	73	6	83	33	66	1s.
Oldcastle,	16	123	18	63	61	6	10	1s.
Trim,	17	91 and 1 to be repaired.	36	15	5 and 1 to be repaired.	17	30	1s.

TABLE I.—RETURN showing what has been done under Improvement Schemes Authorised—*continued.*

Unions.	No. of Electoral Divisions in which the erection of houses has been authorised.	Number of Houses						
		Authorised.	Built.	In Progress.	Not yet commenced.	Abandoned.	Actually Let.	Rent (Weekly).
PROVINCE OF LEINSTER—*continued.*								
QUEEN'S CO.								
Abbeyleix, . . .	9	25	.	.	25	.	.	—
Mountmellick, . . .	11	71	.	.	70	1	.	—
CO. WESTMEATH.								
Delvin, ...	19	161	98	14	44	84	98	About 1s.
Mullingar, . . .	40	204	120	29	47	7	83	10d.
CO. WEXFORD.								
Enniscorthy, . . .	19	93	78	.	1	20	78	10d.
Gorey, ...	23	88	61	.	26	1	60	10d.
New Ross, . . .	10	34	.	.	24	10	.	—
Wexford, . . .	58	372	190	99	.	83	190	1s.
CO. WICKLOW.								
Baltinglass, . . .	11	40	0	28	27	3	6	1s.
Rathdrum, . . .	7	19	10	1	5	6	10	1s. & 1s. 6d.
Shillelagh, . . .	4	16	.	4	12	.	.	—
Total for Leinster, .	435	3,347 and 25 to be repaired.	1,140 and 2 repaired.	475	1,455 and 23 to be repaired.	269	1,089	—
PROVINCE OF CONNAUGHT.								
CO. GALWAY.								
Ballinasloe, . . .	5	8	.	.	8	.		—
Gort, ...	4	5	.	.	5	.		—
Loughrea, . . .	8	16	.	.	16	.		—
CO. LEITRIM.								
Carrick-on-Shannon, .	6	5	4	.	.	1	4	1s.
Manorhamilton, . .	4	17	4	7	5	1	4	1s. 3d. and 1s. 6d.
Mohill, ...	7	17	.	.	17	.	.	—
CO. SLIGO.								
Dromore, West, . .	3	7	6	1	.	.	6	—
Total for Connaught,	37	69	14	8	46	2	14	—
TOTAL FOR ALL IRELAND,	1,209	9,494 and 54 to be repaired.	5,179 and 2 repaired.	1,781 and 11 repairing.	3,255 and 41 to be repaired.	601	4,770	—

TABLE II.—RETURN showing what is proposed to be done under new Improvement Schemes.

NOTE.—This List includes the applications shown as still pending in the Table given at page 24.

UNIONS.	No. of Electoral Divisions comprised in the Schemes.	No. of Cottages proposed to be Built.	Estimated Cost.
PROVINCE OF ULSTER.			£ s. d.
Co. CAVAN.			
Cavan, ...	17	73	6,648 0 0
Total for Ulster, .	17	73	£6,648 0 0
PROVINCE OF MUNSTER.			
Co. CLARE.			
Killadysert, . .	9	74 & 17 to be repaired	8,013 0 0
Co. CORK.			
Macroom, . .	36	370 & 7 to be repaired	77,700 0 0
Millstreet, . .	10	35	3,340 0 0
Mitchelstown, .	15	64 & 1 to be repaired	7,316 0 0
Skibbereen, . .	[illegible]	310	31,000 0 0
Co. KERRY.			
Dingle, . . .	8	75 & 2 to be repaired	8,448 0 0
Kenmare, . .	3	3	315 0 0
Tralee, . . .	35	198	19,840 0 0
Co. LIMERICK.			
Croom, . . .	20	119 & 6 to be repaired	—
Glin, . . .	15	160	16,000 0 0
Kilmallock, . .	[illegible]	477 and 3 acres as allotments.	46,470 0 0
Limerick, . .	[illegible]	204 & 13 to be repaired	26,578 0 0
Rathkeale, . .	16	30 & 18 to be repaired	16,000 0 0
Co. TIPPERARY.			
Cashel, . . .	17	72 and 9 to be repaired.	6,090 0 0
Clogheen, . .	16	133	13,020 0 0
Thurles, . . .	6	66	7,600 0 0
Tipperary, . .	[illegible]	418	41,360 0 0
Total for Munster,	301	2,446, 71 to be repaired, and 3 acres as allotments.	£348,141 0 0
PROVINCE OF LEINSTER.			£ s. d.
Co. KILDARE.			
Athy, . . .	5	11	1,[illegible] 0 0
Celbridge, . .	3	15	—
Co. KILKENNY.			
Castlecomer, . .	3	19	1,900 0 0
Thomastown, . .	9	91	9,100 0 0
Urlingford, . .	16	84	8,400 0 0
KING'S CO.			
Edenderry, . .	19	64	6,[illegible] 15 0
Tullamore, . .	21	121	15,[illegible] 0 0
Co. LOUTH.			
Dundalk, . .	13	47	9,[illegible] 0 0
Co. MEATH.			
Trim, . . .	17	163	16,[illegible] 0 0
QUEEN'S CO.			
Mountmellick, .	31	171	18,[illegible] 0 0
Co. WESTMEATH.			
Mullingar, . .	24	49	7,100 0 0
Co. WEXFORD.			
Enniscorthy, . .	27	117	11,[illegible] 0 0
New Ross, . .	[illegible]	218	21,[illegible] 0 0
Co. WICKLOW.			
Baltinglass, . .	2	8	[illegible] 0 0
Shillelagh, . .	4	41	4,[illegible] 0 0
Total for Leinster,	[illegible]	1,[illegible]	£[illegible] 13 [illegible]
PROVINCE OF CONNAUGHT.			
Co. LEITRIM.			
Carrick-on-Shannon,	3	6	[illegible] 0 0
Co. ROSCOMMON.			
Roscommon, . .	5	7	[illegible] 0 0
Total for Connaught,	8	13	£1,[illegible] 0 0
Total for all Ireland,	[illegible]	3,[illegible], 71 to be repaired, and 3 acres as allotments.	£[illegible],127 [illegible] [illegible]

Housing of the Working Classes Act, 1885.

35. In paragraph 33 of our last Report we gave an account of the proceedings that were being taken under the Labouring Classes Lodging Houses and Dwellings Act of 1860, as incorporated with the Housing of the Working Classes Act of 1885, and since the date of that Report we have sanctioned loans of £7,000 to the Corporation of Kilkenny, £1,600 to the Town Commissioners of Trim, £1,000 to the Corporation of Cork, £685 to the Town Commissioners of Galway, £2,800 to the Town Commissioners of Kinsale, and £2,500 to the Corporation of Wexford.

These sums, together with the sum of £43,825 previously borrowed, constitute a total of £59,410 borrowed up to the 31st March, 1886, by the various Urban Sanitary Authorities in Ireland under the provisions of the Housing of the Working Classes Act.

Applications for loans have been made by the Urban Sanitary Authorities of Enniskillen and Waterford, and are at present under our consideration.

Under the loan of £20,000 granted to the Corporation of Dublin, houses to accommodate about 600 persons have just been completed. The cost, which has not yet been finally ascertained, will, it is estimated, exceed the amount of the loan by £7,000. In Cork seventy-four houses have been erected under the loan of £6,500 granted in 1886, and it is in contemplation to erect sixteen more under the loan granted in 1887. Twenty-five houses have been built in Sligo, and it is intended to build five more immediately. In Trim and Limerick some houses are in course of erection. In the other cases where loans were sanctioned the necessary preliminaries have not yet been completed.

Artizans and Labourers Dwellings Improvement Acts, 1875 to 1885.

36. No Orders have been made under these Acts since the date of our last Annual Report.

Departmental Arrangements.

37. We have to report with much regret the death of Dr. Charles Croker-King, the Medical Commissioner of our Board. The vacancy thus created on the Board has been filled by the appointment of Dr. Francis X. F. MacCabe, late Medical Member of the General Prisons Board, Ireland, and formerly one of our Medical Inspectors. Dr. MacCabe has been succeeded on the Prisons Board by Dr. George Plunkett O'Farrell, one of our Medical Inspectors, and the vacant Inspectorship has been con-

ferred on Dr. Edward C. Thompson, Surgeon of the Tyrone County Infirmary, and Visiting Physician to the Omagh District Lunatic Asylum.

We have also recently been deprived by death of the services of Mr. Æneas M. Byrne, one of our Auditors. Mr. James W. Drury, M.A., Secretary to the Rathmines and Rathgar Township Commissioners, has been appointed to fill the vacancy caused by Mr. Byrne's death.

We have the honour to be,

Your Excellency's obedient servants,

ARTHUR JAMES BALFOUR.
HENRY ROBINSON.
GEORGE MORRIS.
F. X. F. MACCABE.

APPENDIX

TO THE

SIXTEENTH ANNUAL REPORT

OF

THE LOCAL GOVERNMENT BOARD FOR IRELAND.

APPENDIX A.

ORDERS, CIRCULARS, AND CORRESPONDENCE UNDER THE POOR LAW ACTS AND OTHER ACTS NOT INCLUDED IN APPENDIX B OR C.

I.—ORDERS.

No. 1.—General Order Assessing upon Contributory Unions under the National School Teachers Act, their respective proportions of Results Fees for the year ending 31st March, 1888.

To the Guardians of the Poor of the several Unions named in the Schedule to this Order; to the Treasurer of each of such Unions; and to all persons whom it may concern:

Whereas We, the Local Government Board for Ireland, have received from the Commissioners of National Education an estimate for the year ending the 31st day of March, 1888, of the full amount payable as Results Fees in respect of Pupils attending the National Schools in each of the Unions which have become contributory Unions under an Act passed in the Thirty-ninth year of the Reign of Her present Majesty, Queen Victoria, entitled "An Act to provide for additional Payments to Teachers of National Schools in Ireland":

And Whereas the Unions which have become contributory under the said Act are those of which the Names are placed in the first column of the Schedule hereto:

And Whereas by the said Act it is enacted that the Commissioners of National Education shall require the Local Government Board in every year to provide a sum equal to one-third of such full amount payable as Results Fees as aforesaid, and that the said Local Government Board shall thereafter provide such sum in the manner by the said Act prescribed; and the Local Government Board have received from the Commissioners of National Education a requisition to provide, in the year 1887–88, a sum equal to one-third of such full amount aforesaid:

And Whereas it is by the said Act further enacted—"Upon the receipt of every such estimate the Local Government Board shall by an Order under their Seal assess upon each contributory union a sum equal to one-third of the full amount payable as results fees in respect of pupils attending the National Schools in such contributory union, and shall transmit a copy of such order to the guardians and likewise to the treasurer of such contributory union, stating the amount so assessed on such contributory union."

And it is further enacted that "forthwith on the receipt of such order by the treasurer of any contributory union he shall, out of the funds then lying in his hands to the credit of the guardians of such union, or if there shall be then no sufficient assets, out of the moneys next received by him and placed to the credit of such guardians, pay over the amount so assessed on such contributory union to the Bank of Ireland, to be there placed to the credit of the Commissioners of Education to a separate account, to be entitled 'The Results Fees Account:' and that the guardians of such contributory union shall in their account with the electoral divisions of such contributory union debit each electoral division with its proportion of the said amount according to the net annual value for the time being of the property rateable to the rates for the relief of the destitute poor in each such division:"

And Whereas it is provided by the said Act that if in any financial year the sum provided by the Local Government Board in respect of any contributory union exceeds the amount required for the purposes of the Act in such year in respect of such contributory union, such overplus shall be carried to the credit of the next following financial year, and in such last-mentioned year only such sum shall be raised by assessment on such contributory union as shall be necessary in addition thereto to make up the sum which would in the ordinary course under the said Act be required to be provided by the Local Government Board in respect of such contributory union in such next following year:

And Whereas we have received from the Commissioners of National Education a statement of the surplus of previous assessments, as set forth in the fourth column of the Schedule hereto:

Now Therefore, in pursuance of the powers vested in us by the said Act, We do hereby assess upon each of the unions named in the first column of the Schedule hereto the amount set opposite to its name in the fifth column, such sum being equal to one-third of such full amount payable as Results Fees as aforesaid by such union, as set forth in the second column of the said Schedule, less the amount of surplus of previous assessments, as set forth in the fourth column.

SCHEDULE.—CONTRIBUTORY POOR LAW UNIONS.

Name of Union.	Full Amount of Results Fees payable to the Teachers of National Schools situated in Union. (Estimated.)	Amount equal to one-third of the full amount of estimated Results Fees.	Surplus of previous Assessments.	Amount assessed on each Union, being one-third of the full amount of estimated Results Fees less amount of Surplus of previous Assessments.
1st Column.	2nd Column.	3rd Column.	4th Column.	5th Column.
	£ s. d.	£ s. d.	£ s. d.	£ s. d.
Ballymahon, . .	811 8 6	270 9 6	16 9 6	254 0 0
Ballyvaghan, . .	293 15 6	97 11 10	3 11 10	94 0 0
Belfast, . . .	18,121 7 0	6,040 9 0	284 9 0	5,756 0 0
Castlecomer, . .	1,031 0 3	343 13 5	40 13 5	303 0 0
Cloghan, . . .	1,598 7 9	532 15 11	41 15 11	491 0 0
Clogher, . . .	814 0 9	271 6 11	29 6 11	242 0 0
Delvin, . . .	611 14 0	203 18 0	38 18 0	165 0 0
Downpatrick, . .	2,891 4 6	963 14 10	100 14 10	863 0 0
Dungannon, . .	2,089 4 6	696 8 2	25 8 2	671 0 0
Enniskillen, . .	2,541 15 9	847 5 3	66 5 3	781 0 0
Irvinestown, . .	976 16 6	325 12 2	0 12 2	325 0 0
Kells, . . .	1,773 16 0	591 5 4	2 5 4	589 0 0
Listowel, . . .	3,027 0 0	1,009 0 0	—	1,009 0 0
Milford, . . .	859 14 6	286 11 6	5 11 6	281 0 0
Mullingar, . .	2,011 18 0	670 12 8	72 12 8	598 0 0
Navan, . . .	1,694 4 0	564 14 8	21 14 8	543 0 0
Newry, . . .	3,408 0 3	1,136 0 1	148 0 1	988 0 0
Oldcastle, . .	1,093 6 0	364 8 8	14 8 8	350 0 0
Roscrea, . . .	1,212 0 0	404 0 0	—	404 0 0
Strabane, . . .	1,999 15 9	666 11 11	84 11 11	582 0 0
Trim, . . .	1,226 13 0	408 17 8	75 17 8	333 0 0

Sealed with our Seal, this Eleventh day of May, in the year of Our Lord One Thousand Eight Hundred and Eighty-seven.

(Signed), HENRY ROBINSON.
CHARLES CROKER-KING.

LONDONDERRY.

WE, CHARLES STEWART, MARQUESS OF LONDONDERRY, Lord Lieutenant-General and General Governor of Ireland, do hereby approve this Order.

By Command of His Excellency,

REDVERS BULLER.

No. 2.—GENERAL ORDER ASSESSING upon UNIONS in IRELAND the amounts payable by them, respectively, under the Contagious Diseases (Animals) Act.

To the GUARDIANS of the POOR of the several Unions named in the Schedule hereunto annexed; to the Treasurer of each of such Unions, and to all Persons whom it may concern.

WHEREAS, by an Act passed in the Forty-second year of the Reign of Her present Majesty, Queen Victoria, entitled "An Act for making better provision respecting Contagious and Infectious Diseases of Cattle and other Animals, and for other purposes," it is among other things enacted that on receipt of the certificate of the Chief Secretary or Under Secretary to the Lord Lieutenant of Ireland to the effect that a sum equivalent to a certain Poundage, to be specified in such

Certificate, on the net annual value of the property in all the Unions in Ireland, is required for the purposes of the Act, the Local Government Board shall, by order under their Seal, assess that sum on the several Unions, in proportion to the net annual value of the property therein, and the said Board shall transmit copies of the Order to the Guardians and to the Treasurer of each Union:

And Whereas by the said Act it is further enacted that on receipt of such Order, the Treasurer of each Union shall, out of the Union funds, pay over the amount assessed on the Union to the Bank of Ireland, to be placed to the General Cattle Diseases Fund, and the Guardians of each Union shall debit the several Electoral Divisions with proportions of that sum, according to the net annual value of the property therein:

And Whereas it is provided by the said Act that no larger sum shall be levied under the said Act at any one time than shall be equivalent to a poundage of One Halfpenny in the Pound on the net annual value of the property in all the Unions; nor shall any larger sum be levied under the said Act in the whole than shall be equivalent, taken with any money before the commencement of the said Act carried to the Cattle Plague Account, to a poundage of Fourpence in the Pound on the net annual value of the property in all the Unions:

And Whereas a Certificate under the hand of the Chief Secretary to the Lord Lieutenant, bearing date the Twelfth day of May, One Thousand Eight Hundred and Eighty-seven, has been received by Us, the Local Government Board for Ireland, in which it is certified that a sum of Fourteen Thousand Four Hundred and Seventy-seven Pounds Eight Shillings and Four Pence Three Farthings sterling, being equivalent to a rating of One Farthing in the Pound on the net annual value of the property in all the Unions in Ireland, is required for the purpose of the said Act:

Now Therefore, in pursuance of the provisions of the said Act, We, the Local Government Board for Ireland, do hereby assess the said sum of Fourteen Thousand Four Hundred and Seventy-seven Pounds Eight Shillings and Four Pence Three Farthings, upon the several Unions in Ireland, in proportion to the net annual value of the property in each Union according to the Valuation thereof now in force as follows; that is to say, we assess upon each Union the amount set opposite to its name in the Schedule hereunto annexed.

SCHEDULE.

Union.	Amount Assessed. £	s.	d.	Union.	Amount Assessed. £	s.	d.
Abbeyleix,	84	15	4¾	Dromore West,	39	8	5¼
Antrim,	131	1	3¾	Dublin North,	416	5	7¼
Ardee,	98	7	1	Dublin South,	721	17	8½
Armagh,	214	8	5¾	Dundalk,	113	9	3¼
Athlone,	99	1	8¾	Dunfanaghy,	11	19	11¼
Athy,	115	14	10	Dungannon,	99	9	10¼
Bailieborough,	42	0	1¾	Dungarvan,	55	15	10¼
Ballina,	51	18	5¼	Dunmanway,	31	18	0
Ballinasloe,	61	6	11	Dunshaughlin,	110	3	5¾
Ballinrobe,	62	17	1¼	Edenderry,	109	8	5½
Ballycastle,	45	8	8¾	Ennis,	77	5	4½
Ballymahon,	64	11	8¼	Enniscorthy,	115	14	8¼
Ballymena,	138	4	11¼	Enniskillen,	111	14	0
Ballymoney,	90	17	4½	Ennistymon,	39	8	4
Ballyshannon,	53	18	10½	Fermoy,	109	2	4½
Ballyvaghan,	20	13	4½	Galway,	66	13	3
Balrothery,	99	16	8½	Glenamaddy,	33	1	8¾
Baltinglass,	76	17	8¾	Glenties,	81	5	3¾
Banbridge,	165	11	1¾	Glin,	50	12	9¾
Bandon,	76	18	4¾	Gorey,	83	18	10
Bantry,	23	0	5½	Gort,	44	18	9
Bawnboy,	41	11	11¾	Gortin,	30	8	9¼
Belfast,	774	16	3	Granard,	89	7	0¼
Belmullet,	11	6	7¾	Inishowen,	40	14	1
Borrisokane,	43	0	1	Irvinestown,	51	4	11¼
Boyle,	77	5	2¼	Kanturk,	90	11	0½
Cahersiveen,	23	17	9¼	Kells,	100	10	8¼
Callan,	73	6	10¾	Kenmare,	20	7	7
Carlow,	136	9	3	Kilkeel,	48	0	1
Carrickmacross,	32	11	10	Kilkenny,	104	1	8¼
Carrick-on-Shannon,	60	6	5	Killadysert,	30	0	1¼
Carrick-on-Suir,	92	0	11½	Killala,	21	5	7¾
Cashel,	111	12	10¾	Killarney,	78	11	8
Castlebar,	48	9	11¾	Kilmacthomas,	34	19	9½
Castleblayney,	71	0	8½	Kilmallock,	142	12	0½
Castlecomer,	31	10	7¼	Kilrush,	84	19	3
Castlederg,	27	8	6¾	Kinsale,	48	9	10¾
Castlerea,	70	0	7	Larne,	106	5	11¾
Castletown,	18	10	2¼	Letterkenny,	32	17	11
Cavan,	114	15	10¼	Limavady,	79	7	7
Celbridge,	119	8	7¾	Limerick,	206	10	1½
Claremorris,	44	5	6½	Lisburn,	183	10	1
Clifden,	18	5	6½	Lismore,	53	4	1½
Clogheen,	66	1	5¼	Lisnaskea,	60	8	2¾
Clogher,	55	11	4¼	Listowel,	51	3	11
Clonakilty,	53	0	3¼	Londonderry,	170	0	3
Clones,	60	0	4½	Longford,	115	9	2¼
Clonmel,	74	19	2½	Loughrea,	79	9	9½
Coleraine,	108	1	7	Lurgan,	149	19	8¼
Cookstown,	88	3	8½	Macroom,	60	11	3¼
Cootehill,	76	5	1¾	Magherafelt,	99	6	8½
Cork,	371	0	3¾	Mallow,	111	0	11¾
Corrofin,	31	3	11	Manorhamilton,	45	8	2¼
Croom,	69	9	1	Midleton,	98	8	5¼
Delvin,	60	1	4½	Milford,	31	4	6¼
Dingle,	23	16	8	Millstreet,	29	3	10¾
Donegal,	55	17	5½	Mitchelstown,	51	3	0½
Downpatrick,	185	10	10½	Mohill,	41	2	10¾
Drogheda,	130	0	1¾	Monaghan,	99	17	8¼

Schedule—*continued.*

Union.	Amount Assessed.			Union.	Amount Assessed.		
	£	s.	d.		£	s.	d.
Mount Bellow, . .	42	2	2¼	Skull, . . .	19	14	3
Mountmellick, . .	107	1	11½	Sligo, . . .	103	1	4½
Mullingar, . . .	165	0	5	Strabane, . . .	104	9	0
Naas, ...	150	9	8½	Stranorlar, . . .	31	14	1
Navan, ...	125	5	6	Strokestown, . .	53	15	7½
Nenagh, . . .	98	8	1½	Swineford, . . .	42	13	6½
Newcastle, . . .	65	15	6	Thomastown, . .	68	16	4½
New Ross, . . .	105	16	6½	Thurles, . . .	94	6	6½
Newry, ...	177	10	1	Tipperary, . . .	148	14	0½
Newtownards, . .	147	1	10	Tobercurry, . .	43	8	10½
Oldcastle, . . .	83	7	3	Tralee, . . .	91	8	5
Omagh, ...	86	18	0½	Trim, ...	118	9	6½
Oughterard, . .	15	13	1½	Tuam, ...	80	0	9
Parsonstown, . .	107	8	3½	Tulla, ...	34	10	4½
Portumna, . . .	36	19	1½	Tullamore, . . .	65	13	6½
Rathdown, . . .	281	13	6	Urlingford, . . .	50	15	6½
Rathdrum, . . .	136	18	1½	Waterford, . . .	160	5	11
Rathkeale, . . .	66	11	8½	Westport, . . .	46	9	8½
Roscommon, . . .	87	1	11½	Wexford, . . .	113	16	11½
Roscrea, . . .	95	7	3½	Youghal, . . .	62	5	10
Scariff, ...	37	0	5				
Shillelagh, . . .	53	0	9½				
Skibbereen, . . .	46	16	8½	Total, . . £	14,477	6	4½

Sealed with our Seal this Twenty-seventh day of May, in the Year of Our Lord One Thousand Eight Hundred and Eighty-seven.

(Signed), Henry Robinson.
Charles Croker-King.

We, The Lords Justices-General and General Governors of Ireland, do hereby approve this order.

By Command of their Excellencies,

Ashbourne, C. Redvers Buller.

No. 2.—General Order prescribing Forms of Contract for Supplies to be entered into by Boards of Guardians.

The Local Government Board for Ireland.

General Order.

To the Guardians of the Poor of the several Unions named in the Second Schedule hereunto annexed, and the Officers of such Unions; and to all others whom it may concern.

Whereas by Article 20 of our General Order of the 18th day of December, 1882, it is ordered that the contracts mentioned in that Order to be entered into by Guardians of the Poor shall be in such form as We, the Local Government Board for Ireland, may from time to time prescribe or approve, if any form shall have been prescribed or approved by us for that purpose;

Now, Therefore, We, the Local Government Board for Ireland, do hereby prescribe and order, with respect to each and every of the Unions named in the Second Schedule hereunto annexed, that all contracts in writing for the purchase of goods of any kind to be entered into by the Guardians of the Poor of the Union after the date of this order shall, when the goods contracted for are all to be delivered at one time and to be paid for in a single sum, be in the Form No. 1 in the First Schedule hereto; and, when the goods contracted for are to be delivered from time to time in such quantities as shall be required by the said Guardians and paid for accordingly from time to time, shall be in the Form No. 2 in the said First Schedule.

And We do hereby further order and direct that the person or persons so contracting with such Guardians shall in all cases be required to enter, with two Sureties approved of by such Guardians, into a Bond, according to the form of Bond annexed to each form of Contract set out in the First Schedule hereto, in such penal sum as such Guardians shall think fit, conditioned for the due performance of the Contract.

First Schedule.

Form No. 1.

Contract for Supplies.

Memorandum of Agreement, made the day of One Thousand Eight Hundred and BETWEEN of the one part, and the Guardians of the Poor of the Union, of the other part.

It is hereby agreed by and between the said parties hereto; and the said do , in consideration of the payments to be made to as hereinafter mentioned, hereby contract with the said Guardians of the Poor of the Union, that the said shall and will, on or before the day of serve, supply, and deliver, or cause to be delivered, free of all expense, at in the said Union, the following goods, at and after the rates or prices following, that is to say:

And they, the said Guardians of the Poor of the Union, do hereby agree that in case the said shall well and truly serve, supply, and deliver the said Articles, upon the terms, in the manner, and at the time aforesaid, according to this Agreement, they, the said Guardians of the Poor of the Union, shall and will well and truly pay or cause to be paid to the said the rates and prices aforesaid, for the Articles so served, supplied, and delivered, and of which a Bill of Particulars shall be sent with such Articles at the time of the delivery thereof, within days after such delivery.—Provided always, and it is hereby expressly agreed, and particularly by and on the part of the said that in case such Articles shall not be duly served, supplied, and delivered by or when delivered shall not in every respect be of the quality and sort contracted for, and in exact conformity with the patterns or samples exhibited by the said Guardians, or shall be deficient in the weight, size, measure, or quantity stated and charged for in such Bill of Particulars, with such Articles, or if the same shall be delivered without such Bill of Particulars, they the said Guardians, or their Clerk, or other Officer authorized by them, shall be at liberty to return the same at the expense of the said Contractor, or give notice for the same to be sent for and fetched away by And that in every such case it shall be lawful for the said Guardians, or their Clerk, or other Officer authorized by them, to purchase a fresh supply of such Articles, or employ any other person or persons to furnish a fresh supply of such Articles in the place of the said And that in such case the said Executors and Administrators, shall bear and make good all charges, and expenses of such Articles so to be provided, over and above the price at which the same are hereinbefore contracted to be served, supplied, and delivered by the said AND ALSO that it shall be lawful for the said Guardians of the Poor of the Union to retain and apply any sum of money which may be due to the said under and by virtue of this Agreement, at the time of any failure in the performance hereof, to the payment of such charges and expenses as the said Guardians may incur, or be put to by reason thereof. And that, notwithstanding the Agreement hereinbefore contained for making good the Articles which shall not be served, supplied, and delivered according to the terms and in the manner hereinbefore agreed on and in pursuance of this Contract, it shall be lawful for the said Guardians of the Poor of the Union to put in suit the Bond to be given for the performance of this Contract, of even date herewith, against the said and and Sureties, their and each of their Executors or Administrators. PROVIDED ALSO, and it is hereby agreed, that if the said Guardians, with the consent or by direction of the Local Government Board for Ireland, shall at any time during the term of the said Contract, be desirous to put an end to the same, and shall give days' notice thereof in writing to the said or leave such notice at usual place of abode, or of carrying on business, or if in consequence of any rule, order, or regulation of the said Board which may come into effect during the period of such Contract and may affect the performance of the same, the said shall be desirous to put an end to the same, and shall give days' notice thereof, in writing, to the said Guardians or their Clerk, then this present Contract or Agreement shall thereupon in all respects cease and determine, anything herein contained to the contrary thereof in any wise notwithstanding.

And it is hereby further agreed by and between the parties hereto that no action shall be brought nor shall any other proceedings of any kind to enforce payment of the price of any goods supplied in pursuance of this Agreement be taken or commenced after the expiration of three calendar months from the end of the half year in which such goods shall have been supplied, the commencement of such half year to be reckoned from the time up to which the last preceding half-year's accounts shall or ought to have been made up and balanced by the Clerk to the said Guardians, in pursuance of the regulations of the Commissioners for administering the laws for relief of the Poor in Ireland, or of the Local Government Board for Ireland, in force for the time being: Provided that the Local Government Board for Ireland may, if they think fit so to do, by an Order under the Seal of the said Board extend the time within which such action or proceedings may be taken or commenced, for any period not exceeding twelve calendar months after the time when such goods shall have been supplied.

And it is hereby further agreed by and between the parties hereto that no execution of any kind shall be issued, nor shall any judgment, decree or order be enforced, nor shall the amount thereof be levied on foot of, or in respect of the price of any goods supplied in pursuance of this agreement, after the expiration of six calendar months from the end of the half-year aforesaid, unless with the consent of the Local Government Board for Ireland, testified by an Order under the Seal of the said Board.

As Witness the seal of the said Guardians of the Poor of the Union, and the hand of the said the day and year first hereinbefore written.

[*Bond.*]

Know all men by these Presents, That We, are jointly and severally held and firmly bound to the Guardians of the Poor of the Union, in the sum of of good and lawful Money of the United Kingdom of Great Britain and Ireland, to be paid to the said Guardians of the Poor, or their certain Attorney, Successors, or Assigns, for which payment to be well and faithfully made, we bind ourselves jointly, and each of us bindeth himself severally, our and each and every of our Heirs, Executors, and Administrators, and every of them, firmly by these Presents.

Sealed with our Seals. Dated this day of in the year of our Lord One Thousand Eight Hundred and

Whereas, by a certain Contract or Agreement bearing even date with this Obligation, and contained on the two first sides of this sheet, and made between the above-bounden of the one part, and the above-named Guardians of the Poor of the Union of the other part, the said had contracted with the said Guardians of the Poor of the Union aforesaid, to serve, supply, and deliver free of all expense at in the said Union, on or before the day of (such Contract nevertheless to be determinable as in the said Contract or Agreement is mentioned), the several Articles therein specified, of such quality, at such time, and after the rate and price, and subject to the terms, provisions, and stipulations, as in the said Contract or Agreement are particularly mentioned and set forth and as on reference thereto will more fully appear.

Now the condition of this Obligation is such, that if the above-bounden Executors or Administrators, do and shall well and truly perform, fulfil, and keep all and every the covenants, clauses, provisoes, terms, and stipulations in the said recited Contract or Agreement mentioned or contained, and on and their part to be observed, performed, fulfilled, and kept according to the true purport, intent, and meaning thereof, then this Bond or Obligation shall be void, or else shall be and remain in full force and virtue.

Signed, sealed and delivered by the above-bounden [*Seal.*]

[*Seal.*]

in presence of [*Seal.*]

[Form.

FORM No. 2.

Contract for Supplies to be delivered from the day of to the day of

MEMORANDUM OF AGREEMENT, made the day of One Thousand Eight Hundred and BETWEEN of the one part, and the GUARDIANS of the Poor of the UNION, of the other part.

It is hereby agreed by and between the said parties hereto; and the said do in consideration of the payments to be made to as hereinafter mentioned, hereby contract with the Guardians of the Poor of the Union, that the said shall and will, from the day of until the day of next, inclusive, serve, supply, and deliver, or cause to be delivered, free of all expense, at in the said Union, at such times, and in such manner as the said Guardians, or their Clerk, or other Officer of the said Union, duly authorized by them, shall from time to time direct, such quantities of as shall from time to time be required by the said Guardians, at and after the rates or prices following; that is to say,

And they, the said Guardians of the Poor of the Union aforesaid, do hereby agree, that in case the said shall well and truly serve, supply, and deliver the Articles aforesaid, upon the terms and in manner aforesaid, according to this agreement, they, the said Guardians of the Poor of the Union, shall and will well and truly pay or cause to be paid to the said within days after each and every such delivery during said term, at the rates and prices aforesaid, for such quantity of the said Articles as shall have been ordered, served, supplied, and delivered, during said period of and of which a Bill of Particulars shall have been sent at the time of the delivery of said Articles. PROVIDED ALWAYS, and it is hereby expressly agreed, and particularly by and on the part of the said that in case such Articles shall not be duly served, supplied, and delivered by when and as directed by the said Guardians, or their Clerk, or other Officer duly authorized by them, or when delivered shall not in every respect be of the quality and sort contracted for, or shall be deficient in the weight, size, measure, or quantity stated and charged for in such Bill of Particulars, or if the same shall be delivered without such Bill of Particulars, they, the said Guardians, or their Clerk, or other Officer so authorized by them, shall be at liberty to return the same at the expense of the said Contractor, or give notice for the same to be sent for and fetched away by ; and that in every such case it shall be lawful for the said Guardians, or their Clerk, or other Officer so authorized by them as aforesaid, to purchase a fresh supply of such Articles, or of such other Articles in lieu thereof, as the said Guardians, or their Clerk, or other Officer so authorized as aforesaid, shall think fit, or to employ any other person or persons to furnish a fresh supply of such first-mentioned Articles or of such other Articles in lieu thereof, as aforesaid, in such a manner as may be required during the period of the said Contract, or any part of such period in the place of the said
And it is hereby further agreed that in case such first-mentioned Articles shall not be duly served, supplied, and delivered in such quantities as shall from time to time be required by the said Guardians, then in every such case, and as often as it shall so happen, it shall be lawful for said Guardians, or their Clerk, or other Officer so authorized as aforesaid, to purchase from any other person or persons other than such a

supply of the said first-mentioned Articles as shall be necessary to complete the quantity required, or to purchase and provide such quantity or quantities of any other Article or Articles, directed by the said Guardians to be used instead of the said first-mentioned Articles, as shall be considered necessary by the said Guardians to supply such deficiency, and that in any and every of such cases the said Executors and Administrators, shall bear and make good all charges and expenses of such articles so to be provided, over and above the price at which such first-mentioned Articles are hereinbefore contracted to be supplied and delivered by the said

AND ALSO that it shall be lawful for the said Guardians of the Poor of the Union, to retain and apply any sum of money which may be due to the said under and by virtue of this Agreement, at the time of any failure in the performance hereof, to the payment of such charges and expenses as the said Guardians may incur, or be put to by reason thereof; and that, notwithstanding the Agreement hereinbefore contained for making good the Articles which shall not be served supplied, and delivered according to the terms hereinbefore agreed on and in pursuance of this Contract, it shall be lawful for the said Guardians of the Poor of the Union, to put in suit the Bond to be given for the performance of this Contract, of even date herewith, against the said and Sureties, their and each of their Executors or Administrators. PROVIDED ALSO, and it is hereby agreed, that if the said Guardians, with the consent or by direction of the Local Government Board for Ireland, shall at any time during the term of the said Contract, be desirous to put an end to the same, and shall give days' notice thereof, in writing, to the said or leave such notice at usual place of abode, or of carrying on business, or if in consequence of any rule, order, or regulation of the said Board, which may come into effect during the period of such contract and may affect the performance of the same, the said shall be desirous to put an end to the same, and shall give days' notice thereof, in writing, to the said Guardians or their Clerk, then this present Contract or Agreement shall thereupon in all respects cease and determine, anything herein contained to the contrary thereof in anywise notwithstanding.

And it is hereby further agreed by and between the parties hereto that no action shall be brought nor shall any other proceedings of any kind to enforce payment of the price of any goods supplied in pursuance of this Agreement be taken or commenced after the expiration of three calendar months from the end of the half year in which such goods shall have been supplied, the commencement of such half year to be reckoned from the time up to which the last preceding half-year's accounts shall or ought to have been made up and balanced by the Clerk to the said Guardians in pursuance of the regulations of the Commissioners for administering the laws for relief of the Poor in Ireland, or of the Local Government Board for Ireland, in force for the time being: Provided that the Local Government Board for Ireland may, if they think fit so to do, by an Order under the Seal of the said Board extend the time within which such action or proceedings may be taken or commenced, for any period not exceeding twelve calendar months after the time when such goods shall have been supplied.

And it is hereby further agreed by and between the parties hereto that no execution of any kind shall be issued, nor shall any judgment, decree, or order be enforced, nor shall the amount thereof be levied on foot of, or in respect of the price of any goods supplied in pursuance of this agreement, after the expiration of six calendar months from the end of the half-year aforesaid, unless with the consent of the Local Government Board for Ireland, testified by an Order under the Seal of the said Board.

As Witness the seal of the said Guardians of the Poor of the Union, and the hand of the said the day and year first hereinbefore written.

[*Bond.*]

Know all men by these Presents, that We, are jointly and severally held and firmly bound to the Guardians of the Poor of the Union in the Sum of of good and lawful Money of the United Kingdom of Great Britain and Ireland, to be paid to the said Guardians of the Poor of the Union, or their certain Attorney, Successors, or Assigns, for which payment to be well and faithfully made, we bind ourselves jointly and each of us bindeth himself severally, our and each and every of our Heirs, Executors, and Administrators, and every of them, firmly by these Presents. Sealed with our Seals. Dated this day of in the year of our Lord One Thousand Eight Hundred and

Whereas, by a certain Contract or Agreement, bearing even date with this Obligation, and contained on the two first sides of this sheet, and made between the above-bounden of the one part, and the above-named Guardians of the Poor of the Union, of the other part, the said ha contracted with the said Guardians of the Poor of the Union aforesaid, to serve, supply, and deliver, free of all expense, at in the said Union, from the day of to the day of then next inclusive (determinable nevertheless as in the said Contract or Agreement is mentioned), such quantity of the several Articles therein specified as shall be required, of such quality, at such times, and after the rate and price, and subject to the terms, provisions, and stipulations, as in the said Contract or Agreement are particularly mentioned and set forth, and as on reference thereto will more fully appear.

Now the Condition of this Obligation is such, that if the above bounden Executors or Administrators, do and shall well and truly perform, fulfil, and keep all and every the covenants, clauses, provisos, terms, and stipulations, in the said recited Contract or Agreement mentioned or contained, and on and their part to be observed, performed, fulfilled, and kept according to the true purport, intent, and meaning thereof, then this Bond or Obligation shall be void, or else shall be and remain in full force and virtue.

Signed, sealed, and delivered by the above-bounden [*Seal.*]

[*Seal.*]

in presence of [*Seal.*]

SECOND SCHEDULE.

NAMES of the UNIONS to which this ORDER applies.

- Abbeyleix
- Antrim
- Ardee
- Armagh
- Athlone
- Athy
- Bailieborough
- Ballina
- Ballinasloe
- Ballinrobe
- Ballycastle
- Ballymahon
- Ballymena
- Ballymoney
- Ballyshannon
- Ballyvaughan
- Balrothery
- Baltinglass
- Banbridge
- Bandon
- Bantry
- Bawnboy
- Belfast
- Belmullet
- Borrisokane
- Boyle
- Cahirciveen
- Callan
- Carlow
- Carrickmacross
- Carrick-on-Shannon
- Carrick-on-Suir
- Cashel
- Castlebar
- Castleblayney
- Castlecomer
- Castlederg
- Castlerea
- Castletown
- Cavan
- Celbridge
- Claremorris
- Clifden
- Clogheen
- Clogher
- Clonakilty
- Clones
- Clonmel
- Coleraine
- Cookstown
- Cootehill
- Cork
- Corrofin
- Croom
- Delvin
- Dingle
- Donegal
- Downpatrick
- Drogheda
- Dromore West
- Dublin, North
- Dublin, South
- Dundalk
- Dunfanaghy
- Dungannon
- Dungarvan
- Dunmanway
- Dunshaughlin
- Edenderry
- Ennis
- Enniscorthy
- Enniskillen
- Ennistymon
- Fermoy
- Galway
- Glenamaddy
- Glenties
- Glin
- Gorey
- Gort
- Gortin
- Granard
- Inishowen
- Irvinestown
- Kanturk
- Kells
- Kenmare
- Kilkeel
- Kilkenny
- Killadysert
- Killala
- Killarney
- Kilmacthomas
- Kilmallock
- Kilrush
- Kinsale
- Larne
- Letterkenny
- Limavady
- Limerick
- Lisburn
- Lismore
- Lisnaskea
- Listowel
- Londonderry
- Longford
- Loughrea
- Lurgan
- Macroom
- Magherafelt
- Mallow
- Manorhamilton
- Midleton
- Milford
- Millstreet
- Mitchelstown
- Mohill
- Monaghan
- Mount Bellew
- Mountmellick
- Mullingar
- Naas
- Navan
- Nenagh
- Newcastle
- New Ross
- Newry
- Newtownards
- Oldcastle
- Omagh
- Oughterard
- Parsonstown
- Portumna
- Rathdown
- Rathdrum
- Rathkeale
- Roscommon
- Roscrea
- Scariff
- Shillelagh
- Skibbereen
- Skull
- Sligo
- Strabane
- Stranorlar
- Strokestown
- Swineford
- Thomastown
- Thurles
- Tipperary
- Tobercurry
- Tralee
- Trim
- Tuam
- Tulla
- Tullamore
- Urlingford
- Waterford
- Westport
- Wexford
- Youghal

Sealed with our Seal, this Twentieth day of January, in the year of our Lord One Thousand Eight Hundred and Eighty-eight.

(Signed), ARTHUR JAMES BALFOUR.
HENRY ROBINSON.
GEORGE MORRIS.

LONDONDERRY.

We, CHARLES STEWART, Marquess of Londonderry, Lord Lieutenant-General and General Governor of Ireland, do hereby approve this order.

By Command of His Excellency,
WEST RIDGEWAY

No. 4.—General Order prescribing Form of Contract for supplies of Drugs, Medicines, and Medical and Surgical Appliances.

The Local Government Board for Ireland.

General Order.

To the Guardians of the Poor of the several Unions named in the Schedule hereunto annexed, and the Clerks thereof; to the Committees of Management of Dispensary Districts therein; to the Officers of such Districts and to all others whom it may concern.

Whereas, by Article 29 of our General Order made on the 3rd day of November, 1885, We did order that in making Contracts for the supply of Drugs, Medicines, and Medical and Surgical Appliances for the use of a Dispensary in any Union in Ireland, the Board of Guardians of such Union should adopt and make use of the Form of Contract set forth in the said Article, and that the person or persons so contracting should be required to enter with two Sureties, who might be approved by the Board of Guardians, into a Bond, according to the Form of Bond annexed to the said Form of Contract, in such penal sum as the Board of Guardians should think fit, conditioned for the due performance of the Contract:

And Whereas We, the Local Government Board for Ireland, deem it expedient to rescind the said Article of the said General Order and to make this Order in substitution for the said Article;

Now, Therefore, in exercise of the powers vested in Us, We, the Local Government Board for Ireland, Do hereby rescind Article 29 of our said General Order of the 3rd day of November, 1885, and all other rules and orders hitherto made by Us, or by the Commissioners for administering the laws for Relief of the Poor in Ireland, which prescribe the form of such Contracts; and We do hereby order and prescribe that in making all such Contracts as are and were mentioned in the said Article the Guardians of the Poor of each Union shall henceforth adopt and use the Form of Contract hereinafter set forth.

And We do hereby further order and direct that the person or persons so contracting with such Guardians shall in all cases be required to enter, with two Sureties approved of by such Guardians, into a Bond, according to the Form of Bond annexed to the said Form of Contract hereinafter set forth, in such penal sum as such Guardians shall think fit, conditioned for the due performance of the Contract.

FORM OF CONTRACT AND BOND HEREINBEFORE REFERRED TO.

Contract for Supplies of Drugs, Medicines, and Medical and Surgical Appliances, to be delivered from the day of to the day of

Memorandum of Agreement, made the day of One Thousand Eight Hundred and Between of the one part, and the Guardians of the Poor of the Union, of the other part.

It is hereby agreed by and between the said parties hereto; and the said do , in consideration of the Payments to be made to as hereinafter mentioned, hereby contract with the Guardians of the

Poor of the Union, that the said shall and will, from the day of until the day of next, inclusive, serve, supply, and deliver, or cause to be delivered, free of all expense, at in the said Union, at such times, and in such manner as the said Guardians, or their Clerk, or other Officer of the said Union, duly authorized by them, shall from time to time direct, the Articles hereinafter mentioned and described, in such quantities as shall from time to time be required by the said Guardians, and at and after such rates or prices as in the List hereinafter enumerating the said Articles, are set forth;

And they, the said Guardians of the Poor of the Union aforesaid, do hereby agree, that in case the said shall well and truly serve, supply, and deliver the Articles aforesaid, upon the terms and in manner aforesaid, according to said agreement, they, the said Guardians of the Poor of the Union, shall and will well and truly pay or cause to be paid to the said within days after each and every such delivery during said term, at the rates and prices aforesaid, for such quantity of the said Articles as shall have been ordered, served, supplied, and delivered, during said period of and of which a Bill of Particulars shall have been sent at the time of the delivery of said Articles. PROVIDED ALWAYS, and it is hereby expressly declared, agreed, and particularly by and on the part of the said that in case any such Article or Articles as shall or may from time to time be supplied or delivered under the provisions hereof, shall not be considered by the said Guardians in every respect of good quality, and of the quality and sort contracted for, or in exact conformity with the patterns or samples exhibited by or to the said Guardians, then, and in any such case, such questionable Article or Articles shall and may be submitted and referred to some one person, to be named by the Local Government Board for Ireland, whose decision in relation thereto it is hereby agreed shall be final and conclusive upon the parties hereto respectively. And it is hereby further agreed that in the event of any Article or Articles being found and declared by the person so to be named by the said Local Government Board as such referee, not to be in every respect of good quality, or not to be of the quality and sort contracted for, then that the said shall and will thereupon take back such rejected Article or Articles, and shall and will replace the same with other Article or Articles of proper and sufficient quality, according to the true intent and meaning hereof, and shall bear the extra cost of any such Articles as the Guardians shall have been obliged, through such default, to purchase. And it is hereby further expressly agreed, and particularly by and on the part of the said that in case such Articles as are hereby contracted for, or any of them, shall not be duly served, supplied, and delivered by when and as directed by the said Guardians, or their Clerk, or other Officer duly authorized by them, or in case such Article or Articles as shall or may be found and decided by such referee as aforesaid, not to be in every respect of good quality or of the sort contracted for, shall not have been so taken away and replaced by the said as hereinbefore provided, or in case such Article or Articles, or any of them, shall be deficient in the weight, size, measure, or quantity, stated and charged for in such Bill of Particulars, or if the same shall be delivered without such Bill of Particulars, they, the said Guardians, or their Clerk, or other Officer so authorized by them, shall be at liberty to return the same at the expense of the said Contractor, or give notice for the same to be sent for and fetched away by ; and that in every such case the said Guardians, or their Clerk, or other Officer so authorized by them, as aforesaid, may purchase a fresh supply of such Articles, or of such other Articles in lieu thereof, as the said Guardians, or their Clerk, or other Officer so authorized as aforesaid, shall think fit, or employ any other person or persons to furnish a fresh supply of such first-mentioned Articles, or of such other Articles in lieu thereof, as aforesaid, in such a manner as may be required during the period of the said Contract, or any part of such period in the place of the said   And it is hereby further agreed that in case such first-mentioned Articles shall not be duly served, supplied, and delivered in such quantities as shall from time to time be required by the said Guardians, then in every such case, and as often as it shall so happen, the said Guardians, or their Clerk, or other Officer so authorized as aforesaid, may purchase from any other person or persons other than   such a supply of the said first-mentioned Articles as shall be necessary to complete the quantity required, or to purchase and provide such quantity or quantities of any other Article or Articles, directed by the said Guardians to be used instead of the said first-mentioned Articles, as shall be considered necessary by the said Guardians to supply such deficiency, and that in any and every of such cases the said   Executors and Administrators, shall bear and make good all charges and expenses of such Articles so to be provided, over and above the price at which such first-mentioned Articles are hereinbefore contracted to be supplied and delivered by the said   And also that the said Guardians of the Poor of the   Union may retain and apply any sum of money which may be due to the said   under and by virtue of this agreement, at the time of any failure in the performance hereof, to the payment of such charges and expenses as the said Guardians may incur, or be put to by reason thereof. And that, notwithstanding the agreement hereinbefore contained for making good the Articles which shall not be served, supplied, and delivered according to the terms hereinbefore agreed on and in pursuance of this Contract the said Guardians of the Poor of the   Union may put in suit the Bond to be given for the performance of this Contract, of even date herewith, against the said   and Sureties, their and each of their Executors or Administrators. And it is hereby further agreed by and between the parties hereto that no action shall be brought, nor shall any other proceedings of any kind to enforce payment of the price of any goods supplied in pursuance of this agreement be taken or commenced after the expiration of three calendar months from the end of the half-year in which such goods shall have been supplied, the commencement of such half-year to be reckoned from the time up to which the last preceding half-year's accounts shall or ought to have been made up and balanced by the Clerk to the said Guardians in pursuance of the regulations of the Commissioners for administering the laws for relief of the Poor in Ireland, or of the Local Government Board for Ireland, in force for the time being. Provided that the Local Government Board for Ireland may, if they think fit so to do, by an Order under the Seal of the said Board extend the time within which such action or proceedings may be taken or commenced, for any period not exceeding twelve calendar months after the time when such goods shall have been supplied.

And it is hereby further agreed by and between the parties hereto that no execution of any kind shall be issued, nor shall any judgment, decree, or order be enforced, nor shall the amount thereof be levied on foot of, or in respect of the price of any goods supplied in pursuance of this agreement, after the expiration of six calendar months from the end of the half-year aforesaid, unless with the consent of the Local Government Board for Ireland, testified by an Order under the Seal of the said Board.

LIST HEREINBEFORE REFERRED TO.

Articles.	Rates or Prices.

As WITNESS the seal of the said Guardians of the Poor of the Union, and the hand of the said the day and year first herein before written.

[*Bond.*]

KNOW ALL MEN by these Presents, that We, are jointly and severally held and firmly bound to the Guardians of the Poor of the Union, in the Sum of of good and lawful Money of the United Kingdom of Great Britain and Ireland, to be paid to the said Guardians of the Poor of the Union, or their certain Attorney, Successors, or Assigns, for which payment to be well and faithfully made, we bind ourselves jointly, and each of us bindeth himself severally, our and each and every of our Heirs, Executors, and Administrators, and every of them, firmly by these Presents. Sealed with our Seals, and dated this day of in the year of our Lord One Thousand Eight Hundred and

WHEREAS, by a certain Contract or Agreement, bearing even date with this Obligation, and contained on the first two sides of this sheet, and made between the above-bounden of the one part, and the above-named Guardians of the Poor of the Union, of the other part, the said hath contracted with the said Guardians of the Poor of the Union aforesaid, to serve, supply, and deliver, free of all expense, at in the said Union, from the day of to the day of then next inclusive, such quantity of the several Articles therein specified as shall be required, of such quality, at such times, and after the rate and price, and subject to the terms, provisions, and stipulations as in the said Contract or Agreement are particularly mentioned and set forth, and as on reference thereto will more fully appear.

NOW THE CONDITION of this Obligation is such, that if the above-bounden Executors or Administrators, do and shall well and truly perform, fulfil, and keep all and every the covenants, clauses, provisoes, terms, and stipulations, in the said recited Contract or Agreement mentioned or contained, and on and their part to be observed, performed, fulfilled, and kept according to the true purport, intent, and meaning thereof, then this Bond or Obligation shall be void, or else shall be and remain in full force and virtue.

Signed, sealed, and delivered by the above-bounden [*Seal.*]

[*Seal.*]

in presence of [*Seal.*]

SCHEDULE.

NAMES of the UNIONS to which this ORDER applies.

Abbeyleix	Claremorris	Inishowen	Nenagh
Antrim	Clifden	Irvinestown	Newcastle
Ardee	Clogheen	Kanturk	New Ross
Armagh	Clogher	Kells	Newry
Athlone	Clonakilty	Kenmare	Newtownards
Athy	Clones	Kilkeel	Oldcastle
Bailieborough	Clonmel	Kilkenny	Omagh
Ballina	Coleraine	Killadysert	Oughterard
Ballinasloe	Cookstown	Killala	Parsonstown
Ballinrobe	Cootehill	Killarney	Portumna
Ballycastle	Cork	Kilmacthomas	Rathdown
Ballymahon	Corofin	Kilmallock	Rathdrum
Ballymena	Croom	Kilrush	Rathkeale
Ballymoney	Delvin	Kinsale	Roscommon
Ballyshannon	Dingle	Larne	Roscrea
Ballyvaughan	Donegal	Letterkenny	Scariff
Balrothery	Downpatrick	Limavady	Shillelagh
Baltinglass	Drogheda	Limerick	Skibbereen
Banbridge	Dromore, West	Lisburn	Skull
Bandon	Dublin, North	Lismore	Sligo
Bantry	Dublin, South	Lisnaskea	Strabane
Bawnboy	Dundalk	Listowel	Stranorlar
Belfast	Dunfanaghy	Londonderry	Strokestown
Belmullet	Dungannon	Longford	Swineford
Borrisokane	Dungarvan	Loughrea	Thomastown
Boyle	Dunmanway	Lurgan	Thurles
Cahersiveen	Dunshaughlin	Macroom	Tipperary
Callan	Edenderry	Magherafelt	Tobercurry
Carlow	Ennis	Mallow	Tralee
Carrickmacross	Enniscorthy	Manorhamilton	Trim
Carrick-on-Shannon	Enniskillen	Midleton	Tuam
Carrick-on-Suir	Ennistymon	Milford	Tulla
Cashel	Fermoy	Millstreet	Tullamore
Castlebar	Galway	Mitchelstown	Urlingford
Castleblayney	Glennamaddy	Mohill	Waterford
Castlecomer	Glenties	Monaghan	Westport
Castlederg	Glin	Mount Bellew	Wexford
Castlerea	Gorey	Mountmellick	Youghal
Castletown	Gort	Mullingar	
Cavan	Gortin	Naas	
Celbridge	Granard	Navan	

Sealed with our Seal, this Twentieth day of January, in the year of our Lord One Thousand Eight Hundred and Eighty-eight.

(Signed), ARTHUR JAMES BALFOUR.
HENRY ROBINSON.
GEORGE MORRIS.

LONDONDERRY.

WE, CHARLES STEWART, Marquess of Londonderry, Lord Lieutenant-General and General Governor of Ireland, do hereby approve this Order.

By Command of His Excellency.

WEST RIDGEWAY.

No. 5.—ORDER combining the UNIONS of TRIM, DROGHEDA, DUNSHAUGHLIN, NAVAN, and KELLS for the Maintenance and EDUCATION of CHILDREN who are inmates of the Workhouses of such Unions.

To the GUARDIANS of the POOR of the UNIONS of TRIM, DROGHEDA, DUNSHAUGHLIN, NAVAN, and KELLS, and to all others whom it may concern:

WHEREAS, We, the Local Government Board for Ireland, have ascertained that it is expedient to combine the Unions of Trim, Drogheda, Dunshaughlin, Navan, and Kells, for the maintenance and education of children not above the age of 15 years, being inmates of the Workhouses of such Unions respectively:

NOW THEREFORE, We do hereby, in pursuance of the powers vested in Us in that behalf, Order and Declare that the said several Unions of Trim, Drogheda, Dunshaughlin, Navan, and Kells, shall, from and after the Twenty-fifth day of March, 1888, be combined for the maintenance and education of children not above the age of 15 years, being inmates of the Workhouses of the said several Unions respectively. And We do hereby authorize the Guardians of the said Unions, respectively, as and when they shall see fit, to send to a School to be established for the purpose of the maintenance and education of such children, all such children not above the age of 15 years as shall be admitted to the Workhouses of the said Unions, respectively, and to charge the cost of so sending and removing such children to the Electoral Division or to the Union at large, as the case may be, to which relief afforded to such children would by law be chargeable.

AND WE do hereby Order and Direct that a Board of Management for the conduct of such School (hereinafter referred to as the School) shall be established, and that such Board of Management (hereinafter referred to as the Board of Management), shall consist of the Chairman and Six other Guardians of the Trim Union, to be chosen by the Board of Guardians of the said Trim Union in the manner hereinafter prescribed: of the Chairman and Seven other Guardians of the Drogheda Union to be chosen by the Board of Guardians of the said Drogheda Union in like manner; of the Chairman and Six other Guardians of the Dunshaughlin Union to be chosen by the Board of Guardians of the said Dunshaughlin Union in like manner; of the Chairman and Five other Guardians of the Navan Union to be chosen by the Board of Guardians of the said Navan Union in like manner; and of the Chairman and Five other Guardians of the Kells Union to be chosen by the Board of Guardians of the said Kells Union in like manner.

AND WE do hereby Order and Direct that each of the said Unions shall contribute to the cost (hereinafter called the establishment charges) of upholding, repairing, furnishing, and fitting up the School, and of providing articles, implements, and requisites for the common use of the inmates thereof, and of the Staff of the School, in proportion to the annual value of the rateable hereditaments comprised in the said Unions respectively.

AND WE do hereby Order and Direct that the said Unions shall also contribute in proportion to such annual value to the expenses (if any) which may be incurred in hiring or purchasing land or buildings for the purpose of the School, or in building the School, or in altering any building for the purpose of using it for the School.

AND WE do hereby Order and Direct that for each child belonging to the said Unions, respectively, there shall be paid to the said Board of Management a certain sum per diem, to be paid and regulated from time to time in such manner as We shall direct, on account of the maintenance of such child in the School; and such sum, and all other expenses incurred in reference to such child individually, shall be debited to the Electoral Division or Union, as the case may be, to which relief afforded to such child would by law be chargeable.

And We do hereby Order and Direct that at the commencement of every quarter of each year the Board of Management shall cause an estimate to be made of the probable amount of the demand for all charges to be defrayed within such quarter on account of the School; and of the proportion thereof which will be chargeable to the said Unions, respectively, and shall transmit a copy thereof to the Guardians of each of the said Unions, and the Guardians of the said Unions, respectively, within seven days from the receipt of such estimate, shall pay over to the Board of Management the amount therein stated to be chargeable to the said Unions, respectively; and all such payments shall be deemed to be on account of the sums which may be found to be payable to the Board of Management at the close of the half year in respect of the cost of the maintenance of the children according to the daily rate of payment for each child to be fixed and regulated by Us as aforesaid, and in respect of the expenses constituting the establishment and other charges of the School according to the net annual value of the rateable hereditaments comprised in the said Unions respectively as aforesaid; and the balance due, if any, at the close of the half year by the Guardians of the said Unions, respectively, shall be payable to the Board of Management within seven days after notice thereof; and the balance in favour of the Guardians of the said Unions, respectively, if any, shall be carried forward to meet the proportion payable, as hereinbefore directed, of the next quarterly estimate.

And We do hereby Order and Direct that the discharge of any child belonging to any one of the said Unions, and maintained in the School, shall take place only after the removal of such child back to the Union to which it shall belong, and from which it was conveyed to the School.

And We do hereby Order and Direct that the Staff of the School shall be such as We may from time to time authorise and direct.

And We do hereby Order and direct that the several Orders which are now in force for regulating the meetings and proceedings of Boards of Guardians and the appointment and duties of Union Officers, for regulating the management of Workhouses and the duties of Workhouse Officers, for regulating the making and entering into of Contracts, and for regulating the keeping and auditing of accounts, shall, so far as the same are applicable thereto, regulate and govern the proceedings of the Board of Management, the appointment and duties of the Staff of the School, and the keeping of the accounts thereof, as fully as if the said several regulations were set forth in this Order.

And We do hereby Order and Direct that the Guardians to be chosen by the Boards of Guardians of the said Unions respectively, to be Members of the Board of Management, shall be chosen annually at the meeting at which and in the same manner as the Chairman of the said Boards of Guardians are respectively elected, and the Guardians so chosen Members of the Board of Management shall continue to be Members thereof until the next Annual Election of Members of the Board of Management shall take place for their respective Unions, unless they shall previously die, resign, or become incapable, or be disqualified by ceasing to be Guardians of their respective Unions.

And in the event of any vacancy occurring in the Board of Management by reason of any of the causes aforesaid, the Guardians of the Union for which the Guardian so dying, resigning, or becoming incapable or disqualified by ceasing to be a Guardian as aforesaid was chosen, shall within one month after the occurrence of the vacancy, choose some other Guardian to be a Member of the Board of Management in place of the Guardian so dying, resigning, or becoming incapable or disqualified as aforesaid.

Sealed with our Seal, this Twenty-fourth day of February, in the Year of our Lord One Thousand Eight Hundred and Eighty-eight.

(Signed), HENRY ROBINSON.
GEORGE MORRIS.

LONDONDERRY.

We, CHARLES STEWART, MARQUESS OF LONDONDERRY, Lord Lieutenant-General and General Governor of Ireland, do hereby approve this Order.

By Command of His Excellency,
W. RIDGEWAY.

No. 6.—ORDER awarding the amount payable by the PEMBROKE TOWNSHIP to the CORPORATION of DUBLIN in respect of the expense incurred by the Corporation in carrying the PARLIAMENTARY REGISTRATION ACTS into effect in the year 1885.

To the Commissioners of the Township of Pembroke; to the Corporation of Dublin; to the Treasurer of the said Corporation; and to all other Persons whom it may concern.

WHEREAS by Section 12 of the "Parliamentary Registration (Ireland) Act, 1885," it is enacted as follows:—

"The Commissioners of the Townships of Pembroke and Blackrock shall repay to the Treasurer of the Corporation of Dublin so much of the expense incurred by the Corporation in carrying the Parliamentary Registration Acts into effect, in this and every subsequent year, as is properly chargeable to those townships respectively, having regard to the total number of electors registered in that year for the borough of Dublin, and to the number of electors registered in that year for the borough of Dublin in respect of qualifying premises situated in such townships respectively."

"Such payments shall be made by the Commissioners of the said townships out of the rates applicable by them respectively for the general purposes of the township."

"In case any dispute arises as to the amount properly chargeable to either township in any year, it shall be referred to the arbitration of the Local Government Board for Ireland, who, after an inquiry into the matter, at which both the parties shall be entitled to be represented and to give evidence, shall make an award, which shall be binding upon the Corporation of Dublin and upon the Commissioners of such township."

And Whereas a dispute has arisen within the meaning of the said Section as to the amount properly chargeable to the said Township of Pembroke in respect of the expense incurred by the said Corporation in carrying the Parliamentary Registration Acts into effect in the year 1885, and has been referred to the arbitration of the Local Government Board for Ireland who have instituted an inquiry into the matter, at which the said Corporation and the Commissioners of the said Township of Pembroke have been represented and given evidence;

Now therefore, We, the Local Government Board for Ireland, do hereby determine and award that the amount properly chargeable to the said Township of Pembroke in respect of the said expense is One Hundred and Ninety-five Pounds and Fifteen Shillings sterling.

Sealed with our Seal, this Thirtieth day of November, in the Year of our Lord One Thousand Eight Hundred and Eighty-seven.

(Signed), Henry Robinson.
Charles Croker-King.
George Morris.

II.—CIRCULARS.

No. 1.—The "Hessian Fly."

Local Government Board, Dublin,
20th April, 1887.

Sir,

Adverting to their circular letter of the 20th of October last forwarding, for the information of the Guardians, copies of some suggestions made by Mr. Charles Whitehead, F.L.S., F.G.S., for dealing with the Hessian Fly, I am directed by the Local Government Board for Ireland to enclose herewith, to be laid before the Guardians, a copy of a notice which has been issued by the Agricultural Department of the Privy Council Office, London, to County Local Authorities in Great Britain, calling attention to the discovery of the pupa cases of the insect mentioned among the light grains and refuse from threshing machines and upon imported straw.

I am, sir, your obedient servant,
Thos. A. Mooney, Secretary.

To the Clerk of each Union.

Enclosure to the Foregoing.

Notice.

Discovery of the Pupa Cases (Flax Seeds) of the Hessian Fly among the Light Grains and Refuse from Threshing Machines, and upon imported straw.

Pupa Cases of the Hessian Fly have been discovered in considerable numbers among the light grains, and the weed seeds and other refuse from recently threshed wheat and barley.

In view of the urgent importance of preventing the distribution of these Pupa Cases, and their subsequent development into Hessian Flies, in the first warm days of Spring, every means should be adopted at once by Local Authorities to warn agriculturists of this danger.

The light grains and "chogs," and the weed seeds, and all other refuse which fall through the riddles and screens should be carefully examined. If Pupa Cases are found, the light grains and "chogs" should be disposed of, so as to effectually prevent the distribution of the insects; while the weed seeds and other refuse should be burnt.

As Pupa Cases have been found upon imported straw, just above the first or second joint, agriculturists and other purchasers of foreign baled straw should be warned to examine it closely, and if the chestnut-coloured Pupa Cases are seen upon it, to report to the Local Authority, who are requested to transmit the information to the Agricultural Department.

No. 2.—Remuneration of Clerks of Unions for duties under the Parliamentary Voters' Acts.

Local Government Board, Dublin,
22nd April, 1887.

Sir,

The Local Government Board for Ireland have had under consideration the proceedings of Boards of Guardians in regard to payments voted by them from time to time in pursuance of the 73rd Section of the Act 13 & 14 Vic., chap. 69, as compensation to Clerks of Unions for the duties imposed upon them by the Parliamentary Voters' Acts, and to enable them to remunerate the Poor Rate Collectors and other assistants for their services in connection with the discharge of those duties. Resolutions have been proposed and passed in many cases granting such allowances without any previous notice to the Guardians, and it is the opinion of the Board that this course is open to objection.

For several years the same amount was usually paid to the Clerks as remuneration for their services under the Parliamentary Voters' Acts, and as the annual vote was, in most Unions, very much a matter of form it did not appear to be important that the Guardians should be specially summoned to consider the subject, but the sums proposed now in each year vary considerably, and the Board must request that, in future, at least one week's notice may be given to each Guardian before payments are voted under the Act referred to.

I am, sir, your obedient servant,

Thos. A. Mooney, Secretary.

To the Clerk of each Union.

No. 3.—Night Lodgers or "Casuals."

Local Government Board, Dublin,
2nd June, 1887.

Sir,

I am directed by the Local Government Board for Ireland to state for the information of the Board of Guardians that the great increase which has taken place in the number of night lodgers, or casuals, admitted to workhouses in Ireland during the year 1886 has attracted the Board's attention, and that they have obtained reports from their Inspectors respecting the reception and treatment of persons of this class in some workhouses in each province, from which they learn that in many Unions the advice given to Boards of Guardians by the late Poor Law Commissioners in the year 1857, respecting the cleansing, clothing, and searching of such persons, is not attended to.

The Local Government Board have reason to believe that the increase in the number of night lodgers above referred to is attributable in a great measure to applications for temporary relief in workhouses made by labourers and artizans who, in consequence of want of employment in agricultural districts, and the depression in trade, travel about the country seeking for employment, and the Board have no desire that provisional relief should be denied to persons who are really destitute, but they consider that a strict observance of the workhouse rules in dealing with such cases is a matter of much importance, as if lodgings at night in workhouses may be obtained free of expense, without the enforcement of the rules and ordinary discipline of those institutions, facilities are afforded for the adoption of a wandering life, and vagrancy is thus encouraged.

The Local Government Board therefore desire to bring the matter under the notice of the Board of Guardians, and would repeat the advice given to them by the late Poor Law Commissioners in 1857, viz.:—that all persons admitted be subjected to the provisions of the workhouse rules regarding searching, cleansing, and clothing, and also as to discipline and diet, and especially, that no person of the class under consideration be permitted to leave the workhouse without giving three hours' previous notice.

I am, sir, your obedient servant,

Thos. A. Mooney, Secretary.

To the Clerk of each Union.

No. 4.—Outdoor Relief.

Local Government Board, Dublin,
2nd August, 1887.

Sir,

I am directed by the Local Government Board for Ireland to state that the great increase in the number of persons afforded outdoor relief in Ireland during recent years renders it, in the opinion of the Board, very desirable that the Boards of Guardians should give the subject careful consideration, in order that the expenditure under that head may be checked, and the interests of the ratepayers protected.

The Local Government Board invite the attention of the Boards of Guardians to what has taken place in the execution of the Irish Poor Law since it first came into operation in this country in the year 1838. Under the Irish Poor Relief Act of that year relief could only be afforded in the workhouse, and for some years, notwithstanding the occasional existence of much distress, the system was rigidly maintained, but in consequence of the famine with which the country was stricken in the years 1846 and 1847 the workhouses could not contain the number of destitute persons requiring support, and in the autumn of 1847 the administration of outdoor relief was authorised by the Irish Poor Relief Extension Act.

During the continuance of the famine the want of sufficient workhouse accommodation deprived the Boards of Guardians of the power of effectually testing the destitution of applicants, and the number of persons granted outdoor relief was very great and often much in excess of the requirements of the district, but when the condition of the country improved, and additional accommodation was provided, the Boards of Guardians, having become by experience fully sensible of the abuses and imposition attending the outdoor relief system, endeavoured to put an end to it as far as possible, and in a few years the outdoor relief fell to a very low ebb. In the year 1856 the average daily number of persons so relieved was only 920, but since that time there has been a steady increase, and in the year 1866 the average daily number came up to 11,676—in the year 1876 it rose to 30,124—while in the year 1885 it reached 56,434, exclusive of the orphan and deserted children at nurse; these were not years in which exceptional outdoor relief was authorized by the Legislature by reason of severe distress.

From the foregoing remarks it will be observed that, notwithstanding the fact that the population of Ireland during the thirty years in question has decreased by more than one million, the average daily number of persons afforded outdoor relief has increased from 920 to 56,434, while the annual cost of outdoor relief has risen during the same period from £2,245 to £164,951.

In the opinion of the Local Government Board the great increase in this class of relief has been principally brought about by the lax and unsound system under which the Poor Law is administered by Boards of Guardians in many parts of the country.

Experience in the execution of the Poor Law both in England and Ireland has proved conclusively that the direct tendency of any system of outdoor relief is to demoralize the people and absorb the property of the country, and, while temporary outdoor relief in cases of sickness ought to be freely afforded, the practice of permanently relieving persons in that manner in ordinary times, instead of offering them admission to the workhouse, encourages and perpetuates the evils referred to.

It is often alleged that as the outdoor relief afforded to an individual costs less than the maintenance of such pauper in the workhouse the system is economical, but this view of the matter is most erroneous for, while only really destitute persons desire to obtain indoor relief, outdoor relief is eagerly sought for by and often given to persons who ought not to be maintained at the public cost and who would not accept it in the workhouse, and the general expenditure is greatly increased by reason of the excessive number of persons thus supported. No test of destitution has ever been found so thoroughly effectual as the workhouse test, and it is due to those who provide the funds for the support of the poor that proof of the destitution of the applicants for aid should be required and their poverty clearly established, while it cannot be contended that persons who are unable to procure for themselves the necessaries of life have any just or reasonable cause of complaint so long as they can procure effectual relief, or that they are entitled to determine the form and manner in which assistance to them from public funds is to be granted.

The Local Government Board are aware that there are a few Unions in which relief is only given in the workhouse unless in cases of sickness and urgency, and they address the Boards of Guardians of the others in the interests of the ratepayers who are already heavily taxed for purposes other than poor relief. The present seems an opportune time to bring the matter forward as the autumn is the most favourable season of the year for revising the relief lists, and the

Local Government Board hope that the Boards of Guardians who have hitherto afforded outdoor relief very freely will give this important matter their earnest consideration, and endeavour to lessen the charges on the ratepayers by administering the Poor Law Acts on a better and more sound principle than obtains in so many parts of Ireland at present.

I am, sir, your obedient servant,

Thos. A. Mooney, Secretary.

To the Clerk of each Union.

No. 5.—National School Teachers (Ireland) Act.

Local Government Board, Dublin,
30th December, 1887.

Sir,

In pursuance of the 4th Section of "The National School Teachers (Ireland) Act, 1875," the Local Government Board for Ireland transmit to you herewith, to be laid before the Board of Guardians of Union, the Notice which they are required by that Section to transmit, on or before the 1st day of January, to the Guardians of every Union which shall not at such time be a contributory Union within the meaning of the Act.

The Notice now transmitted, as in the case of the Notice which was transmitted on the 30th December, 1880, requires the Guardians within Forty days from the receipt thereof to inform the Local Government Board whether, for the purpose of increasing the remuneration of the Teachers of National Schools within the Union, they are willing to make their Union a contributory Union within the meaning of the Act, and the Guardians will observe therefore that by the present Notice they are now called upon, in pursuance of the requirement of the Act, to decide whether they will become contributory for the year 1888–89 (that is for the year commencing on the 1st April next), and subsequent years, until the resolution to contribute be legally revoked.

The Board forwarded with their Circular of the 30th August, 1875, a copy of the Act, and of various other Documents relating to this subject, and they desire to refer the Board of Guardians to that Circular and the Documents which accompanied it, for any information which they may require before replying to the enclosed Notice.

The Board have to add that the Commissioners of National Education have furnished them with an estimate of the probable amount which will be payable by the Guardians of the several Unions in Result Fees to Teachers of National Schools within the respective Unions for the year 1888–89, and the liability which, according to this estimate, the Guardians will incur by making their Union a contributory one is not expected to exceed £

I am, sir, your obedient servant,

Thos. A. Mooney, Secretary.

To the Clerk,

ENCLOSURE TO THE FOREGOING.

NOTICE.

In pursuance of Section 4 of "The National School Teachers (Ireland) Act, 1875," 38 and 39 Vic., c. 96.

The Guardians of Union are hereby required, within Forty days after the receipt hereof, to inform the Local Government Board for Ireland whether, for the purpose of increasing the remuneration of the Teachers of National Schools within the Union, they are willing to become a contributory Union within the meaning of "The National School Teachers (Ireland) Act," 38 and 39 Vic., c. 96.

By Order of the Board,

THOS. A. MOONEY, Secretary.

30th December, 1887.

III.—CORRESPONDENCE.

DISSOLUTION of BOARDS of GUARDIANS

1.—BELMULLET UNION.—LETTERS TO GUARDIANS.

(1.)

Local Government Board, Dublin,
5th October, 1887.

SIR,

I am directed by the Local Government Board for Ireland to acquaint you, for the information of the Board of Guardians of Belmullet Union, that, having received on the 30th ultimo a communication from the Clerk of the Union notifying to them the fact that no tenders had been received for the half yearly and yearly supply of certain articles of food to the Workhouse, and further that the Guardians had failed to meet on the day upon which the tenders were to have been considered, the Board required the Clerk to summon an extraordinary meeting of the Guardians for the 3rd instant to decide upon the course to be adopted by them under the circumstances.

After the meeting had been held, at which it appears seven Guardians attended, the Board received a report from their Inspector, Captain Sampson, informing them that the Guardians had not at the meeting made any provision for the support of the Workhouse inmates, and that the supply of food then on hands was only sufficient to furnish one meal for the 4th instant.

It seems, therefore, that the Guardians have, notwithstanding the grave responsibility devolving upon them as the persons entrusted with the administration of the Poor Law within the Union, omitted to take the necessary steps for the ordinary support of the inmates within the Workhouse under their charge, and, under these circumstances, the Local Government Board have to state that, unless the Guardians at once proceed to discharge their duty in this respect, the Board will feel it necessary to dissolve the Board of Guardians and to appoint in their stead paid officers to carry into execution the provisions of the Poor Law Acts within the Union.

I am, &c.,

D. J. MACSHEAHAN, Assistant Secretary.

The Presiding Chairman, Board of Guardians,
Belmullet Union.

(2.)

Local Government Board, Dublin,
12th October, 1887.

Sir,

The Local Government Board for Ireland have had before them the Minutes of Proceedings of the Board of Guardians of Belmullet Union on the 8th instant, from which it appears that, notwithstanding the warning contained in the Board's letter of the 5th instant,* the Guardians took no steps to carry on the business of the Union; and the Board now desire to inform the Guardians that, owing to their failure to discharge their duties, the Board deem it necessary to dissolve the Board of Guardians and to appoint paid officers to carry into execution the Poor Law, Medical Charities, and Public Health Acts in the Union.

A copy of the Order dissolving the Board of Guardians is enclosed.

I am, sir, your obedient servant,
Thomas A. Mooney, Secretary.

To the Clerk, Belmullet Union.

Enclosure referred to in the Foregoing.

(Order dissolving Board of Guardians.)

Belmullet Union.

To the Guardians of the Poor of the Belmullet Union; To the Clerk of the said Union; and to all other Persons whom it may concern:

Whereas, through the default of the Board of Guardians of the Belmullet Union, the duties of the Board of Guardians of the said Union have not been duly and effectually discharged according to the intention of the Acts in force for the Relief of the Destitute Poor in Ireland;

Now therefore, We, the Local Government Board for Ireland, do hereby, in exercise of the powers by the said Acts vested in Us in this behalf, declare the said Board of Guardians to be dissolved, and the said Board is hereby dissolved accordingly.

Sealed with our Seal, this Twelfth day of October, in the year of our Lord One Thousand Eight Hundred and Eighty-seven.

(Signed), Henry Robinson.
Charles Crozier-King.
George Morris.

2.—Swineford Union.—Letter to Guardians.

Local Government Board, Dublin,
3rd February, 1888.

Sir,

The Local Government Board for Ireland have had before them the Minutes of Proceedings of the Board of Guardians of Swineford Union on the 24th ultimo, from which they observe that certain contractors for supplies to the workhouse requested payment of their accounts, and stated that unless paid they would stop such supplies, and also the

---

* See page 65.

Minutes of Proceedings of the Guardians on the 31st ultimo, from which the Board find that the Guardians did not on that day make any provision for further supplies.

The Board learn from a report which they have received from their Inspector, Captain Sampson, that the milk and turf contractors have refused to give any further supplies, and that one of the principal contractors has stated that he will not continue to supply after next Tuesday.

The Board also find from a return furnished to them by Captain Sampson that on the 14th ultimo the Guardians owed about £5,900 to contractors and other creditors, in addition to the balance due to the Board of Works in respect of seed rate collected, but not paid.

The Swinford Union having thus been brought under the administration of the Board of Guardians into such a position that supplies cannot be obtained by that body for the due relief of the destitute poor, the Local Government Board deem it necessary to dissolve the Board of Guardians, and to appoint paid officers in their stead.

A copy of an Order to that effect is enclosed.

I am, &c.,

THOS. A. MOONEY, Secretary.

To the Clerk, Swinford Union.

ENCLOSURE REFERRED TO IN THE FOREGOING.

(ORDER DISSOLVING BOARD OF GUARDIANS.)

SWINFORD UNION.

To the GUARDIANS of the POOR of the SWINFORD UNION; to the CLERK of the said Union; and to all other Persons whom it may concern:

WHEREAS, through the default of the Board of Guardians of the Swinford Union, the duties of the Board of Guardians of the said Union have not been duly and effectually discharged according to the intention of the Acts in force for the Relief of the Destitute Poor in Ireland;

NOW THEREFORE, We, the Local Government Board for Ireland, do hereby, in exercise of the powers by the said Acts vested in Us in this behalf, declare the said Board of Guardians to be dissolved, and the said Board is hereby dissolved accordingly.

Sealed with our Seal, this Second day of February, in the year of our Lord One Thousand Eight Hundred and Eighty eight.

(Signed), HENRY ROBINSON.
GEORGE MORRIS.

APPENDIX B.

Medical Charities Act, and Vaccination Acts.

APPENDIX C.

Orders, Circulars, &c., Under Sanitary Acts.

I. Orders.

No. 1.—Applying the Provisions of the General Order of 8th of August, 1879, "Sanitary Order No. III," to the newly constituted Urban Sanitary District of Killiney and Ballybrack.

To the Governing Body of the Township named in this Order; to the Medical Officers of the Dispensary Districts comprised or partly comprised therein; and to all whom it may concern;

Whereas, by a General Order under our Seal, bearing date the Eighth day of August, 1879, We, the Local Government Board for Ireland, did issue Rules and Regulations under the "Public Health (Ireland) Act, 1878," for the Sanitary organization of Urban Sanitary Districts, the said General Order being numbered and described as follows:

"Sanitary Order No. III., relating to Urban Sanitary Districts."

And Whereas, since the issue of the said General Order, We have issued a Provisional Order under our Seal for the constitution of the Township of Killiney and Ballybrack as an Urban Sanitary District, subject to all the Provisions of "The Public Health (Ireland) Act, 1878," "The Public Health (Ireland) Amendment Act, 1879," and "The Public Health (Ireland) Amendment Act, 1884," affecting Urban Sanitary Districts, from and after the confirmation of the Order by Act of Parliament:

And Whereas the said Provisional Order has been duly confirmed by Parliament:

And Whereas it is expedient that the said General Order of the Eighth day of August, 1879, "Sanitary Order No. III., relating to Urban Sanitary Districts," shall apply to and be in force in the Urban Sanitary District above named:

Now Therefore, We do hereby Order and Direct that the said General Order shall apply to and be in force in the Urban Sanitary District above named, as fully and effectually as if the name of the said Urban Sanitary District had been inserted in the Schedule to the said General Order of the Eighth day of August, 1879.

Sealed with our Seal, this Sixth day of August, in the Year of our Lord One Thousand Eight Hundred and Eighty-seven.

(Signed), Henry Robinson.
Charles Croker-King
George Morris.

No. 2.—Cholera Regulations—(Rags from Italy).

To all Coast Guards and Officers of Customs in Ireland, to the Boards of Guardians of Unions, severally acting as Sanitary Authorities on any part of the Coast of Ireland, to all Masters of Ships, and to all other Persons whom it may concern:

Whereas Cholera is now prevalent in certain parts of Italy, and it is expedient that Regulations should be made with reference to Ships having on board bales of Rags from that country:

Now Therefore, We, the Local Government Board for Ireland, do, by this our Order, and in exercise of the power conferred on Us by the Public Health (Ireland) Act, 1878, and every other power enabling Us in this behalf, make the following regulations, and declare that they shall be enforced and executed by the several Authorities specified in the Schedule to our Order dated the 16th day of July, 1883:

Definitions.

Article 1.—In this Order—

The term "Ship" includes vessel or boat:

The term "Coast Guard" includes any person belonging to the Coast Guard having authority from the Lords Commissioners of the Admiralty:

The term "Officer of Customs" includes any person acting under the authority of the Commissioners of Customs:

The term "Master" includes the officer or person for the time being in charge or command of a ship:

The term "Sanitary Authority" means with respect to the seas, rivers, and waters within the limits described in column 1 of the Schedule annexed to the said Order of the 16th day of July, 1883, the Guardians of the Poor of the Unions named in column 3 of the said Schedule, opposite to the descriptions of the said limits respectively:

The term "Port" means a Port established for the purposes of the laws relating to the Customs of the United Kingdom:

The term "Medical Officer of Health" includes any duly qualified Medical Practitioner appointed by a Sanitary Authority to act in the execution of the said Order of the 16th day of July, 1883:

Article 2.—From and after the date of this Order, and until the Thirty-first day of December, 1887, no Rags from Italy shall be delivered overside, except for the purpose of export, or landed in any port or place in Ireland.

Article 3.—If any Rags shall be delivered overside or landed in contravention of this Order, they shall, unless forthwith exported, be destroyed by the person having control over the same, with such precautions as may be directed by the Medical Officer of Health of the Sanitary Authority within whose jurisdiction or district the same may be found.

Article 4.—All Masters of vessels, Consignees, and other persons having control of any Rags prohibited under this Order from being delivered overside, except for the purpose of export, or landed, are required to obey these regulations.

Article 5.—It shall be the duty of the Sanitary Authority to take proceedings against Masters of ships, Consignors, or other persons having control over any Rags, who shall wilfully neglect or refuse to obey or carry out, or shall obstruct the execution of any of these regulations.

Given under our Hands and Seal of Office this Twenty-sixth day of August, in the year of Our Lord One Thousand Eight Hundred and Eighty-seven.

(Signed), HENRY ROBINSON.
CHARLES CROKER-KING.
GEORGE MORRIS.

NOTICE.—The Public Health (Ireland) Act, 1878, provides by Section 148 that any person wilfully neglecting, or refusing to obey or carry out, or obstructing the execution of any regulation made under that Section, shall be liable to a penalty not exceeding *Fifty Pounds*.

No. 3.—MARGARINE ACT, 1887: REGISTRATION OF MANUFACTORIES.

BY THE LOCAL GOVERNMENT BOARD FOR IRELAND.

To the OWNERS and OCCUPIERS for the time being of MANUFACTORIES of MARGARINE in IRELAND to which the Margarine Act, 1887, applies: To the several Local Authorities under the said Act for the time being in Ireland; and to all others whom it may concern.

WHEREAS by Section 9 of the Margarine Act, 1887 (which will come into operation on the 1st day of January, 1888), provision is made for the Registration with the Local Authority of every Manufactory of Margarine (as defined by the said Act) in Ireland from time to time in such manner as We, the Local Government Board for Ireland, may direct:

AND WHEREAS by Section 13 of the said Act the expression "Local Authority" is defined as meaning "any Local Authority authorized to appoint a public analyst under the Sale of Food and Drugs Act, 1875," and the Local Authorities in Ireland authorized to appoint a public analyst under the last named Act are as follows, namely:—The Grand Jury of every County and Town Council of every Borough:

NOW THEREFORE, We, the Local Government Board for Ireland, hereby Order and Direct as follows:—

ARTICLE I.—Every owner or occupier of a Manufactory of Margarine in Ireland who shall make application to the proper Local Authority for a Certificate of Registration under the said Margarine Act, 1887, shall, in his application, state the following particulars:—

(a.) The name and address of the owner or occupier making the application.
(b.) The situation of the manufactory.
(c.) The name and address, or names and addresses, of the owner or owners, or occupier or occupiers, carrying on the manufacture.

Every such application shall be signed by the person making the same, or by some one acting on his behalf.

ARTICLE 2.—If the application is in due form, the Local Authority shall cause the Manufactory to be registered by entering in a Book the particulars of the application for registration; and thereupon a Certificate, in the Form A. set forth in the Schedule hereto, shall be issued by the Local Authority to the person applying for the same.

ARTICLE 3.—Where any change occurs in the persons carrying on the manufacture, written notice thereof shall be given by the owner or occupier of the Manufactory to the Local Authority, and the Register shall thereupon be amended by making therein the requisite alteration, and an endorsement shall be made by the Local Authority on the Certificate in accordance with the Form B. set forth in the said Schedule.

ARTICLE 4.—This Order shall come into operation on the First day of January, One Thousand Eight Hundred and Eighty-eight, and shall remain in force until We shall otherwise direct.

SCHEDULE.

FORM A.

Certificate under the Margarine Act, 1887.
(50 and 51 VICT., c. 29.)

This is to Certify that the Manufactory known as the situate at at which the manufacture of Margarine is at present carried on by the owner [*or occupier*] thereof, has been duly registered by [Here insert the name of the Local Authority within whose District the Manufactory is situate.] in accordance with the provisions of the Margarine Act, 1887, in that behalf, on the application of

Dated this day of , in the Year One Thousand Eight Hundred and Eighty-

Signed,

Clerk to the [Here insert name of Local Authority.]

FORM B.

Endorsement on Certificate in case of Change in Persons carrying on the Manufacture.

This is to Certify that has been duly registered as the owner [or occupier] carrying on the manufacture of Margarine in the within-named Manufactory in the place of

Dated this day of , in the Year One Thousand Eight Hundred and Eighty-

Signed,

Clerk to the [Here insert name of Local Authority.]

Given under our Hands and Seal of Office, this Thirty-first day of December, in the Year of Our Lord One Thousand Eight Hundred and Eighty-seven.

(Signed), ARTHUR JAMES BALFOUR.
HENRY ROBINSON.
GEORGE MORRIS.

II.—CIRCULARS.

No. 1.—STAMPING OF DOCUMENTS.

Local Government Board, Dublin,
3rd September, 1887.

SIR,

The Local Government Board for Ireland have to state, for the information of the Sanitary Authority, that their attention has been drawn by the Controller of Stamps in Ireland to the fact that declarations made by certain Executive Sanitary Officers, in connection with the discharge of duties devolving upon them as such, have been made on forms to which adhesive stamps were affixed instead of on forms bearing impressed stamps, the latter being the only legal kind of stamp applicable in the case of such documents.

The Board have received from the Controller a list showing the documents upon which adhesive stamps may be used, a copy of which is enclosed for the information and guidance of the Sanitary Authority; and they have to request that any declaration or other document upon which duty is payable, not included in the list, which may hereafter be forwarded to the Board by any Officer of the Sanitary Authority, may have the amount of such duty denoted thereon by means of an impressed stamp, in accordance with the legal requirement in such cases.

I am, sir, your obedient servant,
THOMAS A. MOONEY, Secretary.

To the Executive Sanitary Officer,
each Rural and Urban Sanitary
District.

ENCLOSURE TO THE FOREGOING.

The DOCUMENTS for which POSTAGE STAMPS may be used are :—

Agreements liable to a duty of 6*d.*, Bills of Exchange for payment of money on demand liable to the duty of 1*d.*

Certified copies of, or extracts from, Registers of Births, &c. (duty 1*d.*)

Charter Parties (duty 6*d.*)

Contract Notes (duty 1*d.*)

Delivery Orders (duty 1*d.*)

Lease, or Tack, or Agreement, for the Letting, for any definite term less than a year, of a Dwelling-house, or part of a Dwelling-house, at a rent not exceeding the rate of £10 a year (duty 1*d.*)

Lease of a Furnished Dwelling-house, or Apartments, for any definite term less than a year (duties 6*d.*, 1*s.*, 1*s.* 6*d.*, 2*s.*, and 2*s.* 6*d.*)

Letters of Renunciation (duty 1*d.*)

Notarial Acts (duty 1*s.*)

Policies of Insurance (not Life or Marine—duty 1*d.*)

Protests of Bills of Exchange or of Promissory Notes (duties 1*d.*, 2*d.*, 3*d.*, 6*d.*, 9*d.*, and 1*s.*)

Proxies liable to the duty of 1*d.*

Receipts (duty 1*d.*)

Transfers of Shares in Cost Book Mines (duty 6*d.*)

Voting Papers (duty 1*d.*)

Warrants for Goods (duty 3*d.*)

N.B.—Postage Stamps cannot be used for Inland Bills payable otherwise than on demand, for Promissory Notes, for Foreign Bills, for Law or other Fees, nor for any Documents other than those above enumerated.

No. 2.—The Margarine Act, 1887.

Local Government Board, Dublin,
6th January, 1888.

Sir,

I am directed by the Local Government Board for Ireland to draw the attention of the Local Authority to the provisions of the Margarine Act passed during the last Session of Parliament.

It will be observed that Section 9 of the Act referred to requires that every Manufactory of Margarine in Ireland shall be registered by the owner or occupier thereof with the Local Authority, from time to time, in such manner as the Board may direct; and the Board have, accordingly, made an order,* a copy of which is enclosed, directing the manner in which the registration of Manufactories of Margarine is to be made in Ireland.

The term "Local Authority" is defined by Section 13 of the Act to mean any Local Authority authorized to appoint a public analyst under The Sale of Food and Drugs Act, 1875, and Section 10 of the last mentioned Act confers that power, in Ireland, upon the Grand Jury of every County and the Town Council of every borough.

I am, sir, your obedient servant,
Thos. A. Mooney, Secretary.

To the Clerk to the Local Authority.

No. 3.—The Open Spaces Act, 1887.

Local Government Board, Dublin,
16th February, 1888.

Sir,

I am directed by the Local Government Board for Ireland to transmit to you, herewith, for the information of the Sanitary Authority, a copy of The Open Spaces Act† (50 & 51 Vic., cap. 32), passed during the last Session of Parliament, together with copies of the provisions of The Metropolitan Open Spaces Acts, 1877 and 1881, which are extended to Sanitary Districts in England, Wales, and Ireland, by the first mentioned Act.

I am, sir, your obedient servant,
Thos. A. Mooney, Secretary.

To the Executive Sanitary Officer of each Urban and Rural Sanitary District.

---

* See page 70.
† See pages 74, &c.

Enclosure to the Foregoing.

The Open Spaces Act, 1887.

(50 & 51 Vic., Cap. 32.)

together with

The Provisions of the Metropolitan Open Spaces Acts, 1877 and 1881,

Applied to Sanitary Districts Thereby.

---

50 & 51 Vic., c. 32. Open Spaces Act, 1887.

OPEN SPACES ACT, 1887.

---

50 and 51 Vic., Cap. 32.

An Act for extending certain Provisions of the Metropolitan Open Spaces Acts, 1877 and 1881, with Amendments, to Sanitary Districts throughout England, Wales, and Ireland; and for other purposes.
[*23rd August*, 1887.]

40 & 41 Vic., c. 35. 44 & 45 Vic., c. 34. Whereas by the Metropolitan Open Spaces Acts, 1877 and 1881 (herein called the principal Acts), certain facilities were provided for making available the open spaces and burial grounds in the Metropolis for the use of the inhabitants thereof for exercise and recreation, and it is expedient to provide facilities for making available open spaces and burial grounds in all sanitary districts in England, Wales, and Ireland, for the like use of the inhabitants thereof, and to make other provisions for the purpose aforesaid, and also to amend the Metropolitan Open Spaces Act, 1881, and the Disused Burial Grounds Act, 1884.[a] 47 & 48 Vic., c. 72.

Be it therefore enacted by the Queen's Most Excellent Majesty, by and with the advice and consent of the Lords Spiritual and Temporal, and Commons, in this present Parliament assembled, and by the authority of the same, as follows:—

Interpretation. 1. In this Act, unless the context otherwise requires, the expression "urban sanitary district" and the expression "urban authority" respectively, and the expressions "rural sanitary district" and "rural authority" respectively shall have the meanings assigned to them respectively by the Public Health Act, 1875.[b] 38 & 39 Vic., c. 55.

Amendment of 44 & 45 Vic., c. 34. 2. (1.) The Metropolitan Open Spaces Act, 1881,[c] is hereby repealed to the extent mentioned in the schedule to this Act, and the second section of the said Act is hereby amended, as follows (that is to say), the purchase money paid for or in respect of the purchase of any open space as therein mentioned shall be held in trust, either as in the said section mentioned, or as the case may be, for the benefit of the objects to which any rates previously imposed in respect of such open space had been applied.

(2.) The playing of any games or sports shall not be allowed in any churchyard, cemetery, or burial ground in or over which any estate, interest, or control is acquired under section five of the Metropolitan Open Spaces Act, 1881.[d]

Provided that—

(a.) In the case of consecrated ground, the bishop, by any license or faculty granted under the Metropolitan Open Spaces Act or this Act, and

---

[a] This Act applies to England only.

[b] See section 18.

[c] See page 79.

[d] See page 53.

(*b.*) In the case of any churchyard, cemetery, or burial ground which is not consecrated, the body from which any such estate, interest, or control as aforesaid is acquired

may expressly sanction any such use of the ground, and may specify any conditions as to the extent or manner of such use.

Provision as to removal of tombstones and monuments.

3. In the case of any disused churchyard, cemetery, or burial ground,[a] at least three months before any tombstone or monument is moved, the following steps shall be taken:

(*a.*) A statement shall be prepared sufficiently describing by the name and date appearing thereon the tombstones and monuments standing or being in the ground, and such other particulars as may be necessary;

(*b.*) Such statements shall be deposited with the clerk of the board or vestry, and shall be open to inspection by all persons;

(*c.*) An advertisement of the intention to remove or change the position of such tombstones and monuments shall be inserted three times at least in some newspaper circulating in the neighbourhood of the burial ground, and such advertisement shall give notice of the deposit of such statement as is hereinbefore described, and of the hours within which the same may be inspected;

(*d.*) A notice in terms similar to the advertisement shall be placed on the door of the church (if any) to which such churchyard, cemetery, or burial ground is attached, and shall be delivered or sent by post to any person known or believed by the board or vestry to be a near relative of any person whose death is recorded on any such tombstone or monument.

In the case of any consecrated ground no application for a faculty shall be made until the expiration of one month at least after the appearance of the last of such advertisements as aforesaid.

Provided that on any application for a faculty, nothing shall prevent the bishop from directing or sanctioning the removal of any tombstone or monument if he is of opinion that reasonable steps have been taken to bring the intention to effect such removal to the notice of some person having a family interest in such removal.

Amendment of 47 & 48 Vic. c. 72.

4. In the Disused Burial Grounds Act, 1884,[b] and this Act, the expression "burial ground" shall have the same meaning as in the Metropolitan Open Spaces Act, 1881,[c] as amended by this Act, and the expression "disused burial ground" shall mean any burial ground which is no longer used for interments, whether or not such ground shall have been partially or wholly closed for burials under the provisions of any statute or Order in Council, and the expression "building" shall include any temporary or movable building.

Extension of certain provisions of Metropolitan Open Spaces Acts to urban and certain rural sanitary districts.

5. All the provisions of the principal Acts[d] as amended by this Act (except sections four, five, six, seven, and eight of the Metropolitan Open Spaces Act, 1877, and so much of section six of the Metropolitan Open Spaces Act, 1881, as begins with the words "byelaws made under this Act" and ends with the figures "1855," and also except sections ten, eleven, twelve, and thirteen of the last-mentioned Act), shall extend and be applicable to and in respect of any and every urban sanitary district, and any and every rural sanitary district in respect of which the sanitary authority shall have been invested by an order of the Local

[a] See section 4 of this Act. [b] This Act applies to England only.

[c] See § 1 of 44 & 45 Vic., cap. 34 (page 70).

[d] I.e., 40 & 41 Vic., cap. 35 (page 75), and 44 & 45 Vic., cap. 34 (page 78).

50 & 51 Vic., c. 32. Open Spaces Act, 1887.

Government Board with the powers of this Act, and to the open spaces and burial grounds in such districts respectively; and for the purposes of such extension and application to every such district, every urban authority and every such rural authority shall have and may exercise, and there shall be vested in such authority in and for its district, all and every or any such powers, authorities, and capacities in respect of, or in relation to, open spaces or burial grounds within such district as the Metropolitan Board of Works, herein called the Metropolitan Board,[a] by virtue of the principal Acts as amended by this Act have or may exercise or enjoy with regard to open spaces or burial grounds within the Metropolis or any of them; and for the purposes of this Act and in respect of any and every open space or burial ground within any such sanitary district, and of any and every such authority, the principal Acts shall be read and take effect as if the word "Metropolis" when used therein meant the same sanitary district, and as if the words "Metropolitan Board" and "Board" when used therein meant the sanitary authority of the same district, and as if the words "any two or more London daily papers," whenever they occur therein, meant "any two or more local newspapers circulating within the sanitary district."

6.[b] . . . .

Power of Corporations to make free gift of land for open space.

7. Any corporation other than municipal corporations or body of persons having power, either with or without the consent of any other corporation or body of persons, to sell land belonging to such corporation or body may, but with the like consent (if any), convey for valuable or nominal consideration or by way of gift, to any urban or rural authority such land, or any part thereof, for the purpose of the same being preserved as an open space for the enjoyment of the public, and may so convey the same with or without conditions, and the urban or rural authority may accept such open space, and, if conditions are imposed, subject to such conditions, and such open space shall be deemed to be an open space within the meaning of the principal Acts and this Act.

Where a corporation having power under this section to convey land are themselves the urban or rural authority, this section shall enable such authority to appropriate their land for an open space, and shall, with the necessary modifications, apply to such appropriation in like manner as it applies to the conveyance.

Expenses.

8. (1.) All expenses incurred under this Act by an urban or a rural authority shall be deemed to have been incurred in the execution of the Public Health Act, 1875,[c] and shall be defrayed accordingly, and the purposes of this Act, shall be deemed to be the purposes of the Public Health Act, 1875.[c]

(2.) Provided that the expenses incurred by a rural authority shall be deemed to be special expenses under that Act incurred in respect of the contributory place or places for which the powers of this Act are exercised, and all the provisions of the Public Health Act, 1875,[c] which would be applicable in the case of an apportionment of special expenses for works for the common benefit of two or more contributory places, shall apply to any such expenses.

Saving for Crown lands.

9. This Act shall not extend to any land belonging to Her Majesty in right of her Crown or of Her Duchy of Lancaster, or to any garden or ornamental ground for the time being under the management of the Commissioners for the time being of Her Majesty's Works and Public Buildings.

---

[a] See latter part of this section. See also section 13.
[b] This section does not apply to Ireland.
[c] See section 13 of this Act.

10. All the provisions with respect to byelaws contained in sections one hundred and eighty-two to one hundred and eighty-six (both inclusive) of the Public Health Act, 1875,[a] shall apply to all byelaws from time to time made by an urban or rural authority under the powers of this Act, and the penalties imposed by any such byelaws may be recovered in a summary manner.

50 & 51 Vict., c. 32, Open Spaces Act, 1887.

Byelaws.

11. The Metropolitan Board or the sanitary authority may exercise all the powers given to them by the Metropolitan Open Spaces Act, 1881,[b] or this Act respecting open spaces, churchyards, cemeteries, and burial grounds transferred to them in pursuance of the said Act or of this Act in respect of any open spaces, churchyards, cemeteries, and burial grounds of a similar nature which are or shall be vested in them in pursuance of any other statute, or of which they are otherwise the owners.

Power over open spaces already vested in sanitary authority.

12. The Metropolitan Board[a] may purchase or take on lease, lay out, plant, improve, and maintain lands for the purpose of being used as public walks or pleasure grounds, and may support or contribute to the support of public walks or pleasure grounds provided by any person whomsoever.

Power of Metropolitan Board with respect to public walks or pleasure grounds.

13. The principal Acts[c] and this Act shall apply to Ireland, subject to the following provisions:—

Extension of Acts to Ireland.

In the said Acts—

References to the Public Health Act, 1875, shall be construed as references to the Public Health (Ireland) Act, 1878, and the reference to sections one hundred and eighty-two to one hundred and eighty-six of the first-mentioned Act shall be construed as referring to sections two hundred and nineteen to two hundred and twenty-three of the latter Act.

41 & 42 Vic., c. 52.

Reference to any private or local Act of Parliament shall be construed so as to include any Act of the Parliament of Ireland.

References to a "vestry," "district board," "corporation," or "Metropolitan Board," shall be construed as references to the sanitary authority.

References to the London daily papers shall be construed as references to any newspapers, daily or weekly, circulating within the district of the sanitary authority.

References to Her Majesty's Council shall be construed as references to Her Majesty's Privy Council in Ireland.

References to the Local Government Board shall be construed as references to the Local Government Board for Ireland.

References to the Lands Clauses Act, 1845, shall be construed as references to that Act, as amended by the Lands Clauses Consolidation Acts Amendment Act, 1860, the Railways (Ireland) Act, 1851, the Railways (Ireland) Act, 1860, the Railways (Ireland) Act, 1864, and the Railways Traverse Act.

23 & 24 Vic., c. 106. 14 & 15 Vic., c. 70. 23 & 24 Vic., c. 97. 27 & 28 Vic., c. 71. 31 & 32 Vic., c. 70.

Nothing contained in the principal Acts[c] or in this Act shall apply to any land for the time being under the management of the Commissioners

---

[a] See section 13 of this Act.

[b] See page 78.

[c] i.e. 40 and 41 Vic., cap. 35 (page 75), and 44 and 45 Vic., cap. 34 (page 79).

50 & 51 Vic., c. 32, Open Spaces Act, 1887.

of Public Works in Ireland, or belonging to the Benchers of the King's Inns in Dublin.

Short title and construction.

14. This Act may be cited as the Open Spaces Act, 1887, and may be read with the principal Acts as one Act.

SCHEDULE.

Portions of the Metropolitan Open Spaces Act, 1881, repealed.

In section one, the following words occurring in the definition of an "open space," viz., "but shall not include any enclosed land which has not a public road or footpath completely round the same."

In the same section, the following words occurring in the definition of a "burial ground," viz., "and in which interments have taken place since the year 1800."

In the second paragraph of section five, the words, "but such metropolitan board, vestry, or district board shall not allow the playing of any games or sports therein."

---

40 & 41 Vic., c. 35. Open Spaces (Metropolis) Act, 1877.

OPEN SPACES (METROPOLIS.)

40 and 41 Vic, Cap. 35.

An Act for affording Facilities for the enjoyment by the Public of Open Spaces in the Metropolis. [2nd August, 1877.]

Whereas it is expedient to afford facilities for making available the open spaces in and near the metropolis[a] for the use of the inhabitants for exercise and recreation, and to enable the Metropolitan Board of Works[a] to acquire the control and management of such open spaces for such purposes;

Be it enacted by the Queen's most Excellent Majesty, by and with the advice and consent of the Lords Spiritual and Temporal, and Commons, in this present Parliament assembled, and by the authority of the same, as follows:

Metropolitan Board of Works may acquire and hold open spaces for benefit of public.

1. The Metropolitan Board of Works[a] may, by purchase on voluntary sale, or by the gift of the person or persons legally entitled to dispose of the same, acquire or accept the ownership of any open spaces, whether inclosed within rails or palings, or un-inclosed, situated in the metropolis, and hold the same in trust for the perpetual use thereof by the public for exercise and recreation, and may from time to time make byelaws for the regulation of such open spaces, and may by such byelaws provide for the removal of any person infringing any such byelaw by any officer of the said Board, or police constable. Byelaws[b] under this section shall be made in the same manner and subject to the same conditions as byelaws made by the said Board under the Metropolis Management Act, 1855.

18 & 19 Vic., c. 120.

---

[a] See sections 5 and 13 of 50 and 51 Vic., cap. 32 (pages 76 and 77).

[b] See section 10 of the Act 50 and 51 Vic., cap. 32, as to provisions with respect to Byelaws made by an Urban or Rural Sanitary Authority under the powers of that Act (page 77).

2. Where any open spaces now are or hereafter may be used as places of exercise and recreation for the inhabitants of certain houses, and the property and right of user is now or hereafter may be vested in one or more persons as owners or occupiers of such houses, such owners and occupiers (if any) may convey to the Metropolitan Board of Works[a] in trust for the public, the right to enter upon and use and enjoy such open spaces, subject to such terms and conditions as may be agreed upon. 40 & 41 Vic., c. 35. Right of entry to places of recreation may be conveyed to Metropolitan Board of Works.

3. The Metropolitan Board of Works[a] shall be entitled to make such provision as may be necessary for maintaining and protecting the open spaces so acquired by them. Provision for keeping up open spaces.

. . . .

METROPOLITAN OPEN SPACES ACT, 1881.

44 & 45 Vic., Cap. 34.

44 & 45 Vic., c. 34, Metropolitan Open Spaces Act, 1881.

An Act to amend the Metropolitan Open Spaces Act, 1877.

[11th August, 1881.]

Whereas by the Metropolitan Open Spaces Act, 1877,[b] certain facilities were provided for making available the open spaces in the metropolis for the use of the inhabitants thereof for exercise and recreation, and it is expedient to amend and extend the said Act, and to provide greater facilities for the purpose aforesaid: 40 & 41 Vic., c. 35.

Be it enacted by the Queen's most Excellent Majesty, by and with the advice and consent of the Lords Spiritual and Temporal, and Commons, in this present Parliament assembled, and by the authority of the same, as follows:

1. In this Act, unless the context otherwise requires— Interpretation clause.

"Open space" means any land (whether inclosed or uninclosed) which is not built on, and which is laid out as a garden or is used for purposes of recreation, or lies waste and unoccupied;[c]

. . . .

"The metropolis" means the metropolis as defined by the Metropolis Management Act, 1855; 18 & 19 Vic., c. 120.

"The Metropolitan Board" means the Metropolitan Board of Works as constituted by the same Act;

"Vestry"[d] means a vestry of one of the parishes specified in Schedule A of the same Act;

"District board"[d] means a board of works of one of the districts specified in Schedule B of the same Act;

---

[a] See sections 8 and 12 of 50 and 51 Vic., cap. 32 (pages 76 and 77.)

[b] See page 73.

[c] Omitted portion repealed. See section 2 of 50 and 51 Vic., cap. 32 (page 74), and schedule to that Act (page 76).

[d] See section 13 of 50 and 51 Vic., cap. 32 (page 77).

44 & 45 Vic., c. 34. Metropolitan Open Spaces Act, 1881.

"The corporation"[a] means the mayor and commonalty and citizens of the city of London, and the powers conferred upon them by this Act may be exercised by the mayor, aldermen, and commons of the said city in common council assembled;

The "owner" of a churchyard, cemetery, or burial ground means the person or persons, corporation sole, or body corporate in whom the soil and freehold of such churchyard, cemetery, or burial ground is vested, whether as appurtenant or incident to any benefice or cure of souls, or otherwise.

The term "burial ground" shall include any ground, whether consecrated or not, which has been at any time set apart for the purposes of interment.[b]

. . . .

Power to trustees to transfer certain open spaces to local authority.

2. Where any open space within the metropolis is under the provisions of any Private or Local Act of Parliament placed under the care and management of trustees or other persons, with a view to the preservation and regulation of the same as a garden or open space, it shall be lawful for the said trustees or other the managing body thereof for the time being, in pursuance of any resolution duly passed as hereinafter mentioned, and with the consent, to be signified in manner hereinafter appearing, of the owners and occupiers of any houses fronting upon, or the owners or occupiers of which are liable to be specially rated for the maintenance of the open space, to convey, assign, or transfer for valuable or nominal consideration, or by way of gift, to the Metropolitan Board,[c] or to the vestry[c] or district board[c] of the parish or district in which such open space or any part thereof is situate, the soil and freehold of, or other their entire interest in, or (where no interest in the soil of such open space is vested in them) the entire care and management of the said open space, to the end that the same may be preserved for the enjoyment of the public; and upon such conveyance, assignment, or transfer such trustees or other managing body shall be relieved and discharged from all trusts, powers, and duties imposed upon them by the Act or other instrument under which they were constituted, or under which they then act or otherwise with reference to the said open space, but shall hold any purchase money paid for or in respect of the said open space in trust for the benefit of the persons or class of persons for whose benefit the said open space was previously preserved and managed by the said trustees,[c] and such persons or class of persons shall be discharged from any special rate or other obligation previously imposed on them in respect of such open space.

It shall be lawful for any such trustees or managing body as aforesaid, in pursuance of any such resolution as aforesaid, and with such consent as aforesaid, for any valuable or nominal consideration, by way of rent or otherwise, or without any consideration, to grant or transfer to the Metropolitan Board,[c] or to any such vestry or district board as aforesaid, any term of years or other limited interest in or any right or easement over such open space, or to enter into any agreement with the Metropolitan Board[c] or any such vestry[c] or district board[c] as aforesaid for the opening to the public of such open space, and the care and management thereof by such board or vestry at all times or at any specified time or times, without the transfer to such board or

---

[a] See section 13 of 50 and 51 Vic., cap. 32 (page 77).
[b] Omitted portion repealed. See section 2 of 50 and 51 Vic., cap. 32 (page 74), and schedule to that Act (page 78).
[c] See amendment contained in section 1 of 50 and 51 Vic., cap. 32 (page 74).

vestry of any interest in the soil of such open space; and any such grant, demise, transfer, or agreement as aforesaid shall be deemed a good execution of the trusts, powers and duties imposed upon the said trustees by the Act or other instrument under which they are constituted or act. 44 & 45 Vic., c. 34, Metropolitan Open Spaces Act, 1881.

A resolution under this section shall be deemed to have been duly passed if at a meeting of the trustees or other the persons constituting such managing body as aforesaid, summoned by at least one month's notice in writing left at or sent by post to their last known or usual place of abode, such resolution shall have been passed by a majority of two thirds in number of the persons present at such meeting, and if such resolution shall also have been confirmed by two thirds in number of the persons present at a second like meeting, to be summoned by such notice as aforesaid, and to be held at an interval of not less than one calendar month from the first meeting.

The consent of such owners and occupiers of houses as aforesaid shall be held to have been given and signified if, at a meeting of such persons summoned by at least one month's notice in writing given as hereinafter directed, a resolution shall have been passed by a majority of at least two-thirds in number of the persons present at such meeting consenting to the conveyance, grant, or transfer of the said open space as aforesaid, or to such an agreement with the Metropolitan Board,* vestry,* or district board,* as aforesaid; and if such resolution shall also have been confirmed by two-thirds in number of such owners and occupiers present at a second like meeting, to be summoned in like manner to the first meeting, and to be held at an interval of not less than one calendar month from the first meeting.

Notice of such meeting shall be given by leaving the same or sending the same through the post to every house fronting upon, or the owner or occupier of which is liable to be specially rated for the maintenance of, the said open space, and by inserting the same as an advertisement at least three times in any two or more London daily papers,* and such notice shall state generally the object of the said meeting, and no such meeting shall be held between the first day of August in one year and the thirty-first day of January in the following year.

For the purposes of this section the owner of a house shall include any person entitled to any term of years therein; and the occupier of a house shall be the person rated to the relief of the poor in respect of the said house.

If at any meeting of such trustees or managing body, or at any meeting of such owners or occupiers as before mentioned, the resolution proposed at any such meeting be not carried, no meeting shall be called or held with the same object in respect to the same garden or open space until the expiration of three years from the day on which such resolution so proposed was rejected at any such meeting as above mentioned.

A conveyance, assignment, demise, grant, or agreement under this section shall be made by an instrument under the common seal of the trustees or other managing body if such body be a corporation, and if it be not a corporation under the hands and seals of any five members of such body, or of all the members thereof if for the time being they be less than five in number.

The trustees or other the managing body of any such open space as aforesaid may (anything contained in the Act or other instrument under

44 & 45 Vic., c. 34, Metropolitan Open Spaces Act, 1881.

which they are constituted or act to the contrary notwithstanding), in pursuance of any such resolution as aforesaid, and with such consent as aforesaid, signified as aforesaid, admit persons not owning, occupying, or residing in any house fronting on the said open space to the enjoyment of the said open space at all times, or at any specified time or times, and may regulate the admission of such persons thereto on such terms and conditions in all respects as the trustees may think proper.

Any trustees so acting as aforesaid shall have the same power of making byelaws[a] as that conferred by the fourth section of the Act passed in the twenty-sixth year of Her Majesty, chapter thirteen, intituled "An Act for the protection of certain garden or ornamental grounds in cities and boroughs" upon the committee therein mentioned.

Where the freehold of any such open space as is referred to in this section, and the freehold of all or of the major part of the houses round such open space are vested in the same person or persons, the powers conferred by this section shall not be exercised without the consent of such person or persons.

Power to transfer other open space to local authority.

3. The owner of any open space within the metropolis which is subject to rights of user for exercise and recreation (secured by covenant or otherwise) in the owners and occupiers (or either of such classes) of any houses round or near the same may, with the consent (to be signified in manner hereinafter appearing) of such owners and occupiers of houses, convey to the Metropolitan Board,[b] or to the vestry[b] or district board[b] of the parish or district in which such open space or any part thereof is situate, the soil of the said open space in trust for the enjoyment of the public; and the owner or any person or persons in whom any term of years or other limited interest in such open space is vested may, with the like consent, grant or transfer to the Metropolitan Board[b] or such vestry[b] or district board[b] as aforesaid, in trust as aforesaid, any term of years or other limited interest in or any right or easement over such open space, or enter into any agreement with the Metropolitan Board[b] or any such vestry[b] or district board[b] as aforesaid for the opening to the public of such open space, and the care and management thereof by such board or vestry either at all times or at any specified time or times without the transfer to such board or vestry of any interest in the soil of such open space.

The consent of such owners and occupiers of houses as aforesaid shall be held to have been given and signified if at a meeting of such persons summoned by at least one month's notice in writing (given as hereinafter directed) a resolution shall have been passed by a majority of at least two-thirds in number of the persons present at such meeting consenting to the conveyance, grant, or transfer of the said open space as aforesaid, or to such an agreement with the Metropolitan Board,[b] vestry,[b] or district board[b] as aforesaid, and the owner shall be thereupon discharged from any liability to any person entitled to such right of user as aforesaid in respect of any act done in accordance with such resolution.

Notice of such meeting shall be given by leaving the same or sending the same through the post to every house, the owner or occupier of which is entitled to any right of user, and by inserting the same in an

---

[a] See section 10 of the Act 50 and 51 Vic., cap. 32, as to provisions with respect to Bye-laws made by an Urban or Rural Sanitary Authority under the powers of that Act (page 77).

[b] See section 13 of 50 and 51 Vic., cap. 32 (page 77).

advertisement at least three times in any two or more London daily papers,[a] and such notice shall state generally the object of the said meeting; and no such meeting shall be held between the first day of August in one year and the thirty-first day of January in the following year.

44 & 45 Vic., c. 34. Metropolitan Open Spaces Act, 1881.

For the purposes of this section the owner of an open space shall be any person or persons in whom the soil of the open space is vested for an estate in possession during his or their life or lives or for any larger estate; the owner of a house shall include any person entitled to any term of years therein; and the occupier of a house shall be the person rated to the relief of the poor in respect of the said house.

Power to transfer disused burial grounds to local authority.

4. The owner of any churchyard, cemetery, or burial ground situate within the metropolis, and closed for burials either under an order of Her Majesty the Queen in Council,[a] or otherwise, may convey the soil of such churchyard, cemetery or burial ground, or grant any term of years or other limited interest therein to or enter into any agreement with the Metropolitan Board[a] or the vestry[a] or district board[a] of the parish or district in which such churchyard, cemetery, or burial ground, or any part thereof, is situate for the purpose of giving the public access to the said churchyard, cemetery, or burial ground, and preserving the same as an open space accessible to the public, and under the control of such board or vestry, and for the purpose of improving and laying out the same.

Powers and duties of local authority.

5. The Metropolitan Board[a] and the vestry[a] or district board[a] of the parish or district within which any open space, churchyard, cemetery, or burial ground, or any part thereof, is situate, may, by agreement, and for valuable or nominal consideration by way of payment in gross or of rent, or otherwise, or without any consideration, take and hold the soil and freehold of, or any term of years or other limited estate or interest in, or any right or easement in or over any open space, churchyard, cemetery, or burial ground, and may, with reference to any open space, churchyard, cemetery or burial ground, undertake the entire or partial care, management, and control thereof, whether any interest in the soil is transferred to the board or vestry or not, and may for the purposes aforesaid enter into any agreement with the persons authorized by this Act to agree with reference to any open space, churchyard, cemetery, or burial ground or with any other persons interested therein.

Any estate or interest in or control over any open space, churchyard, cemetery, or burial ground acquired by the Metropolitan Board,[a] or any vestry,[a] or district board[a] under the provisions of this Act, shall be held and administered by such board or vestry in trust to allow, and with a view to, the enjoyment by the public of such open space, churchyard, cemetery, or burial ground in an open condition, free from buildings and under proper control and regulation, and for no other purpose,[b] . . . . and the board or vestry shall maintain and keep the same in a good and decent state, and may inclose or keep the same inclosed with proper railings and gates, and may drain, level, lay out, turf, plant, ornament, light, seat, and otherwise improve the same, and do all such works and things, and employ such officers and servants, as may be requisite for the purposes aforesaid, or any of them.

---

a See section 18 of 50 and 51 Vic., cap. 32 (page 77).

b Omitted portion repealed. See section 2 of 50 and 51 Vic., cap. 32 (page 74), and schedule to that Act (page 78).

44 & 45 Vic., c. 34, Metropolitan Open Spaces Act, 1881.

Provided that no board[a] or vestry[a] shall exercise any of the powers of management in this Act mentioned with reference to any consecrated ground, unless and until they are authorised so to do by the license or faculty in that behalf of the bishop of the diocese in which such consecrated ground is situate, which license or faculty may be granted by such bishop upon the application of the board or vestry, and may extend to the removal of any tombstone or monument, under such conditions and subject to such restrictions as to the bishop may seem fit.

Byelaws.

6. The Metropolitan Board[a] and any vestry[a] or district Board[a] may, with reference to any open space, churchyard, cemetery, or burial ground in or over which it has acquired any estate, interest, or control under the provisions of this Act, make byelaws[b] for the regulation thereof, and of the days and times of admission thereto, and the preservation of order and prevention of nuisances therein, and may by such byelaws[b] impose penalties for the infringement thereof, and provide for the removal of any person infringing any such byelaw by any officer of the board or vestry or police constable.

. . . .

Metropolitan Board and vestry or district board may carry out Act jointly.

7. The Metropolitan Board[a] or any vestry[a] or district board,[a] and where an open space extends into two or more parishes or districts two or more vestries or district boards, either with or without the Metropolitan Board, may jointly carry out the provisions of this Act, and may enter into any agreement, on such terms as may be arranged between them, for so doing and for defraying the expenses of the execution of the Act, and the Metropolitan Board may defray the whole or any part of the expenses of the execution of this Act by any vestry or district board, and any vestry or district board may similarly defray the whole or any part of the expenses of the Metropolitan Board or, where an open space extends into two or more parishes or districts, of any other vestry or district board.

Provision for extra-parochial places.

8. Where any open space, churchyard, cemetery, or burial ground, by virtue of any Act of Parliament or otherwise, is extra-parochial, or forms part of some parish other than that which surrounds the same, the vestry[a] or district board[a] acting for the parish surrounding the same may carry out, or may enter into agreement with any one or more vestries or district boards acting for any other parishes, on such terms as may be arranged between them, and may jointly carry out, the provisions of this Act, and shall have the same powers in every respect as if such open space, churchyard, cemetery, or burial ground were part of the parish or district of such vestry or district board.

Provision for compensation.

9. No estate, interest, or right of a profitable or beneficial nature in, over, or affecting an open space, churchyard, cemetery, or burial ground shall, except with the consent of the body or person entitled thereto, be taken away or injuriously affected by anything done under this Act without compensation being made for the same; and such compensation shall be paid by the Metropolitan Board,[a] vestry,[a] or district board[a] by which such estate, interest, or right is taken away or injuriously affected, and shall, in case of difference, be ascertained and provided in the same manner as if the same compensation were for the compulsory purchase and taking or the injurious affecting of lands under the provisions of the Lands Clauses Consolidation Act, 1845, and any Acts amending the same.

8 & 9 Vic., c. 18.

10. . . . .

---

[a] See section 18 of 50 and 51 Vic., cap. 32 (page 77).

[b] See section 10 of 50 and 51 Vic., cap. 32 (page 77).

No. 4.—INSURANCE OF LABOURERS' DWELLINGS.

Local Government Board, Dublin,
23rd March, 1888.

SIR,

The Local Government Board for Ireland desire to state that their attention has been directed to some cases in which Sanitary Authorities have omitted to insure labourers' dwellings provided by them under the Labourers (Ireland) Acts, and, although the Board presume that this precautionary measure has been generally adopted, they think it desirable to impress upon the Sanitary Authorities of the several Unions in which Improvement Schemes have been authorized to be carried into execution the importance of effecting and maintaining an insurance on each cottage built, or acquired, by them for the purposes of the Acts in question.

I am, sir, your obedient servant,

THOS. A. MOONEY, Secretary.

To the Clerk
Union.

APPENDIX D.

TABLES CONNECTED WITH POOR RELIEF AND EXPENDITURE.

No. 1.—A Return (in pursuance of the 29th Section of the Act 10 Vic., cap. 31) Relieved in and out of the Workhouses, together with the Receipts in each Expenditure under the Medical Charities and Vaccination Acts, the National School Teachers, and the Parliamentary Voters, Jurors, and Explo- Poor Rates during the Year.

Part 1.—Return showing the Receipts and Expenditure

Names of Counties and Towns.	Receipts.					[illegible]	Expenditure.			
	Amount of Poor Rate	Parliamentary Grant	Other Receipts, including repayment of Relief	Amount of	Total Receipts during the Year,		In-Maintenance	Out-Relief	[illegible]	[illegible]

of the EXPENDITURE on the RELIEF of the POOR, and of the TOTAL NUMBERS UNION in IRELAND, for the Year ended 29th September, 1887; also showing the Registration, Public Health, Superannuation, Labourers, Contagious Diseases (Animals) cives Acts; the amount of LOANS repaid, and the TOTAL EXPENDITURE out of the

PART I.—RETURN showing the Receipts and Expenditure of Unions during the Year ended 29th September, 1887—*continued.*

Names of Counties and Unions.	Expenditure—(continued).			Amount of Expenditure included in Columns 74 and 77 defrayed out of Loans.		[illegible]	Valuation on 29th Sept., 1887.	Poundage on the Valuation.	
	Expenses under the Public Health (Ireland) Acts, and Sanitation Acts.	Repayment of Loans.	Total Expenditure [illegible]	Poor Relief.	Other Expenditure.			[illegible]	[illegible]
[illegible]	75.	76.	77.	78.	79.	80.	81.	82.	83.
PROVINCE OF ULSTER.	£	£	£	£	£	£	£	s. d.	s. d.
ANTRIM.									
Antrim,	265	19	6,3[illegible]	-	319	-	120,097	0 7½	0 10½
Ballycastle,	74	-	2,[illegible]	-	-	-	41,[illegible]	0 9½	0 11½
Ballymena,	375	-	6,79[illegible]	-	-	-	1[illegible]	0 8	1 0
Ballymoney,	100	470	4,07[illegible]	-	190	-	83,104	0 7½	1 1
Belfast,	1,890	1,098	81,875	-	-	-	786,461	0 11½	1 4
Larne,	116	360	6,127	-	1,083	-	102,104	0 8	1 2
Lisburn,	201	43	4,415	-	-	-	176,980	0 5½	0 7½
ARMAGH.									
Armagh,	180	190	6,837	-	-	-	201,[illegible]	0 6½	0 7½
Lurgan,	290	80	8,149	-	-	-	1[illegible],816	0 9½	1 1½
CAVAN.									
Bailieborough,	99	-	3,391	-	-	-	40,378	1 1½	1 8
Bawnboy,	721	97	3,[illegible]	60	-	172	30,119	1 1	1 7½
Cavan,	160	114	11,118	-	2,971	14	110,[illegible]	0 11½	1 4
Cootehill,	108	-	3,026	-	-	-	73,101	0 9½	0 10
DONEGAL.									
Ballyshannon,	180	84	3,419	-	-	-	30,[illegible]	1 6½	1 6
Donegal,	104	-	2,[illegible]	-	-	-	34,128	0 10	1 3½
Dunfanaghy,	62	46	1,873	-	-	91	11,[illegible]	1 3	[illegible]
Glenties,	75	9	3,[illegible]	-	-	8	20,111	1 1½	[illegible]
Inishowen,	131	171	6,[illegible]	-	-	-	3[illegible]	1 3½	[illegible]
Letterkenny,	164	-	2,[illegible]	-	-	-	51,578	0 11	1 4
Milford,	141	60	2,[illegible]	-	-	-	[illegible]	0 10½	1 3½
Stranorlar,	95	-	1,[illegible]	-	-	-	30,[illegible]	0 8	1 [illegible]
DOWN.									
Banbridge,	280	-	6,016	-	-	-	150,[illegible]	0 7½	0 9½
Downpatrick,	194	160	6,976	-	-	-	170,[illegible]	0 4½	0 8
Kilkeel,	75	121	2,[illegible]	-	-	-	61,[illegible]	0 7	1 1½
Newry,	263	285	10,[illegible]	-	-	-	1[illegible]	0 9½	1 3½
Newtownards,	265	-	7,118	-	-	-	141,[illegible]	0 7½	1 0
FERMANAGH.									
Enniskillen,	310	290	6,[illegible]	-	98	-	1[illegible]	0 9	1 1
Irvinestown,	75	35	2,711	-	-	-	60,171	0 7	1 1½
Lisnaskea,	87	87	2,718	-	-	-	58,[illegible]	0 7	0 11½
LONDONDERRY.									
Coleraine,	210	251	7,056	-	1,[illegible]	-	101,[illegible]	0 9	1 0
Limavady,	98	810	3,[illegible]	-	-	-	[illegible]	0 6½	0 7½
Londonderry,	209	-	6,[illegible]	-	-	-	1[illegible]	0 8½	0 9½
Magherafelt,	196	-	4,219	-	-	-	83,[illegible]	0 7½	0 11½
MONAGHAN.									
Carrickmacross,	64	-	2,[illegible]	-	-	-	60,177	0 10½	1 3
Castleblayney,	79	-	4,1[illegible]	-	-	-	75,[illegible]	0 9½	1 1
Clones,	121	-	2,776	-	-	-	67,[illegible]	0 5½	0 8
Monaghan,	185	-	3,[illegible]	-	-	-	94,[illegible]	0 6½	0 8
TYRONE.									
Castlederg,	116	53	1,[illegible]	-	-	-	27,446	0 8	1 3
Clogher,	104	-	2,811	-	-	-	64,107	0 7	1 0
Cookstown,	120	300	4,[illegible]	-	-	-	65,418	0 0	1 0
Dungannon,	284	1,[illegible]	6,778	-	1,[illegible]	-	1[illegible],618	0 7½	1 0
Gortin,	125	-	1,418	-	-	-	16,[illegible]	0 10½	1 [illegible]
Omagh,	244	-	3,[illegible]	-	-	-	98,175	0 7½	1 0
Strabane,	314	289	4,[illegible]	-	-	-	100,336	0 7½	1 4
Total, Ulster. 1887,	8,[illegible]	9,105	242,318	60	7,781	[illegible]	4,3[illegible]	0 8½	1 1½
Total, Ulster. 1886,	6,157	7,7[illegible]	2[illegible],451	-	1,3[illegible]	1,[illegible]	4,3[illegible],171	0 8½	1 1½
Increase,	2,[illegible]	4[illegible]	6,761	60	6,475	-	18,1[illegible]	-	-
Decrease,	-	-	-	-	-	1,0[illegible]	-	0 0½	-

PART I.—RETURN showing the Receipts and Expenditure of Unions during the Year ended 29th September, 1887—*continued.*

Names of Counties and Unions.	Receipts. Amount of Poor Rate Lodged.	Parliamentary Grant.	Other Receipts (including repayments of Relief by way of Loan, &c.)	Amount of Loans.	Total Receipts during the Year, exclusive of Seed Rate.	Seed Rate Lodged.	Expenditure—(continued). In-Maintenance.	Out-Relief.	[illegible]	Emigration Expenses.
1.	2.	3.	4.	5.	6.	7.	8.	9.	10.	11.
PROVINCE OF MUNSTER.	£	£	£	£	£	£	£	£	£	£
CLARE.										
Ballyvaughan, .	2,084	85	86	-	2,299	-	948	172	26	5
Corrofin, .	2,[illegible]	140	4	116	2,648	8	441	109	7	8
Ennis, .	8,787	877	65	1,117	10,818	-	6,380	1,443	69	16
Ennistymon, .	3,678	197	43	-	4,387	-	2,301	894	65	22
Killadysert, .	3,467	231	5	70	3,784	1	1,026	888	11	16
Kilrush, .	6,448	377	60	-	7,190	-	2,373	2,270	42	4
Scariff, .	2,785	144	11	-	3,391	-	1,161	877	67	17
Tulla, .	4,[illegible]	153	94	-	4,497	-	1,683	624	59	-
CORK.										
Bandon, .	6,673	644	78	6,100	11,783	-	1,943	3,189	80	7
Bantry, .	6,013	347	36	-	3,419	-	768	672	35	-
Castletown, .	1,833	264	18	-	2,363	-	767	151	-	-
Clonakilty, .	4,217	784	48	80	4,454	-	1,677	842	60	16
Cork, .	49,205	2,397	1,308	440	62,791	-	16,230	14,137	1,368	88
Dunmanway, .	2,461	264	7	-	2,627	-	901	645	68	21
Fermoy, .	3,794	687	126	573	7,184	-	1,701	1,578	60	85
Kanturk, .	8,756	681	40	245	11,480	-	2,917	2,455	64	-
Kinsale, .	3,680	273	165	960	4,467	-	1,620	181	16	-
Macroom, .	7,167	646	66	-	7,770	-	2,366	3,574	35	28
Mallow, .	9,823	1,185	386	8,835	13,369	-	2,780	2,167	83	17
Midleton, .	8,261	739	58	480	9,271	-	2,710	2,158	70	-
Millstreet, .	5,019	734	31	880	6,263	-	1,687	482	-	38
Mitchelstown, .	4,779	188	138	680	6,282	-	1,790	482	65	-
Skibbereen, .	6,341	377	11	6,000	7,779	114	4,329	1,173	56	69
Skull, .	7,516	140	6	883	8,869	3	971	493	41	16
Youghal, .	6,074	438	50	8,410	6,283	-	2,095	3,184	166	6
KERRY.										
Cahersiveen, .	4,139	650	31	800	4,820	83	703	682	73	-
Dingle, .	3,416	407	48	-	3,414	-	1,453	161	44	1
Kenmare, .	3,401	351	86	-	3,734	7	883	1,083	23	-
Killarney, .	9,716	845	35	-	10,604	-	3,601	2,477	216	55
Listowel, .	6,518	481	178	415	7,498	-	1,401	2,215	76	50
Tralee, .	9,[illegible]	853	329	6,445	18,[illegible]	130	3,482	8,504	183	32
LIMERICK.										
Croom, .	4,687	150	170	2,111	6,784	-	1,481	1,880	43	6
Glin, .	3,110	251	72	410	4,225	-	1,169	1,781	41	13
Kilmallock, .	10,311	478	821	16,150	21,715	-	5,446	4,104	364	70
Limerick, .	21,797	2,767	878	3,510	30,341	-	16,317	6,071	801	11
Newcastle, .	7,176	783	377	150	7,810	-	1,893	2,311	74	84
Rathkeale, .	8,243	498	176	1,945	10,286	-	1,465	3,286	67	35
TIPPERARY.										
Borrisokane, .	3,801	198	93	-	3,885	-	718	441	16	-
Carrick-on-Suir, .	5,113	398	31	85	5,911	-	1,713	748	14	4
Cashel, .	9,113	785	131	4,431	13,960	-	3,217	2,800	168	14
Clogheen, .	6,871	409	113	140	6,171	-	1,887	131	61	-
Clonmel, .	6,091	350	277	770	9,818	-	3,161	1,570	88	13
Nenagh, .	6,947	480	915	1,893	9,813	-	2,711	3,407	38	-
Roscrea, .	6,071	447	41	-	6,593	-	1,548	815	80	-
Thurles, .	6,901	391	92	-	7,394	-	2,315	3,226	77	8
Tipperary, .	13,166	480	274	16,970	30,974	44	4,464	4,711	128	-
WATERFORD.										
Dungarvan, .	4,891	862	894	2,719	8,743	-	3,891	1,251	66	18
Kilmacthomas, .	2,036	345	18	-	3,317	-	1,214	748	16	10
Lismore, .	3,980	443	107	1,900	9,440	-	1,341	180	28	5
Waterford, .	11,315	1,140	865	3,200	17,866	-	4,811	3,451	191	46
Total, Munster, 1887.	354,035	25,[illegible]	7,114	83,660	478,784	870	178,151	68,[illegible]	4,379	191
Total, Munster, 1886.	347,770	29,461	7,861	71,778	462,[illegible]	9,715	[illegible]	63,[illegible]	4,[illegible]	[illegible]
Increase, .	6,535	-	-	11,876	16,[illegible]	-	-	4,927	-	67
Decrease, .	-	3,913	641	-	-	9,185	3,409	-	40	-

(*continued.*

PART I.—RETURN showing the Receipts and Expenditure

Names of Counties and Unions.	[continued.] Expenditure. Salaries and Rations of Officers.	All other Poor Relief Expenditure.	Total Poor Relief Expenditure.	Expenses under Medical Charities and Vaccination Acts.	Expenses under the Acts for Registration of Births, Deaths, and Marriages.	Expenses under the Public Health Act. For Sanitary purposes.	For Burial Grounds.	[illegible]	Expenses under the Labourers Acts.	[illegible]	[illegible]
12.	13.	14.	15.	16.	17.	18.	19.	20.	21.	22.	23.
PROVINCE OF MUNSTER.	£	£	£	£	£	£	£	£	£	£	£
CLARE.											
Ballyvaghan,	370	384	1,[illegible]	129	6	165	1	36	-	25	14
Corrofin,	316	320	1,[illegible]	177	11	80	12	94	78	31	-
Ennis,	1,115	889	7,[illegible]	784	43	318	201	122	346	15	-
Ennistymon,	877	615	4,[illegible]	441	41	688	13	33	-	43	-
Killadysert,	428	[illegible]	2,[illegible]	200	23	77	17	-	300	44	-
Kilrush,	1,030	657	4,[illegible]	804	78	351	155	10	3	77	-
Scariff,	475	358	3,270	493	25	178	6	-	48	47	-
Tulla,	515	370	3,[illegible]	363	28	165	7	-	331	60	-
CORK.											
Bandon,	783	605	4,305	713	31	2,320	-	84	488	120	-
Bantry,	871	330	1,779	620	26	201	15	-	-	43	-
Castletown,	405	174	1,[illegible]	319	25	118	11	80	-	26	-
Clonakilty,	624	673	3,402	487	11	193	-	-	179	80	-
Cork,	4,[illegible]	6,[illegible]	11,[illegible]	4,[illegible]	331	1,[illegible]	107	620	861	650	79
Dunmanway,	495	278	1,620	384	31	101	4	713	108	3	-
Fermoy,	1,231	725	5,[illegible]	1,[illegible]	65	369	29	62	844	136	-
Kanturk,	871	720	[illegible]	1,031	49	373	45	207	-	142	14
Kinsale,	590	585	2,136	1,031	44	807	14	159	68	105	-
Macroom,	[illegible]	550	3,317	864	32	264	39	149	740	74	-
Mallow,	1,071	904	7,[illegible]	1,360	47	640	713	101	1,756	188	-
Midleton,	800	1,036	4,[illegible]	971	46	1,324	24	134	740	154	-
Millstreet,	587	467	3,482	463	27	177	18	149	148	36	-
Mitchelstown,	613	463	3,351	508	37	140	85	18	718	70	-
Skibbereen,	741	941	5,280	831	50	372	41	234	305	38	-
Skull,	286	299	1,770	1,171	26	86	28	4	67	16	-
Youghal,	610	670	4,[illegible]	761	26	185	6	77	1,616	154	-
KERRY.											
Cahersiveen,	597	768	2,[illegible]	759	65	871	38	91	-	63	13
Dingle,	535	700	2,311	777	45	180	70	107	11	19	-
Kenmare,	544	281	2,[illegible]	614	30	170	23	60	3	39	-
Killarney,	1,149	1,103	7,[illegible]	1,171	57	680	33	520	-	183	26
Listowel,	713	615	5,456	797	50	604	26	69	188	137	26
Tralee,	1,780	1,329	9,[illegible]	1,[illegible]	57	483	77	135	2,675	183	-
LIMERICK.											
Croom,	853	611	4,870	567	23	676	10	79	1,737	148	6
Glin,	465	374	3,[illegible]	442	23	600	18	68	1,320	76	-
Kilmallock,	1,776	1,411	15,[illegible]	1,[illegible]	71	1,417	85	624	11,677	263	-
Limerick,	2,783	4,[illegible]	21,[illegible]	1,[illegible]	145	485	67	398	8,073	380	-
Newcastle,	760	684	4,[illegible]	814	57	388	28	11	721	175	-
Rathkeale,	754	654	6,380	730	31	354	25	-	1,390	154	40
TIPPERARY.											
Borrisokane,	418	382	1,[illegible]	440	18	110	-	84	960	73	-
Carrick-on-Suir,	823	798	4,[illegible]	781	47	181	100	105	897	189	-
Cashel,	1,262	1,011	9,[illegible]	804	56	283	-	77	4,350	163	-
Clogheen,	716	870	3,413	560	37	157	8	9	1,018	137	287
Clonmel,	1,281	1,379	6,7[illegible]	1,075	36	211	7	48	981	84	-
Nenagh,	880	489	5,[illegible]	881	78	315	-	180	[illegible]	152	-
Roscrea,	747	787	3,718	790	40	212	2	214	-	116	60
Thurles,	730	687	4,117	1,113	56	262	-	65	-	139	-
Tipperary,	1,139	1,071	11,570	1,[illegible]	73	443	70	77	12,820	80	-
WATERFORD.											
Dungarvan,	820	832	6,[illegible]	630	31	161	4	185	41	114	-
Kilmacthomas,	520	185	2,[illegible]	308	15	183	-	45	1,175	79	-
Lismore,	670	605	3,[illegible]	630	21	900	5	79	2,142	80	-
Waterford,	2,012	1,[illegible]	16,[illegible]	1,604	130	854	60	161	4,115	273	-
Total Munster, [illegible]	44,916	47,422	390,578	44,579	2,676	18,650	2,411	6,179	78,413	6,[illegible]	1,[illegible]
Total Munster, [illegible]	44,311	42,[illegible]	387,[illegible]	41,618	2,711	22,[illegible]	2,[illegible]	[illegible]	60,[illegible]	6,[illegible]	[illegible]
Increase,	272	-	2,604	960	-	-	115	102	18,033	2,[illegible]	187
Decrease,	-	304	-	-	102	9,[illegible]	-	-	-	-	-

Year ended 29th September, 1887—*continued.*

Amount of Expenditure included in Columns 15 and 16 defrayed out of Loans. Poor Rate.	Other Expenditure.	Amount repaid in Contributions of Public Works Loans	Valuation, 1886.	Percentage on the Valuation.	
17.	18.	19.	30.	31.	32.
£	£	£	£	s. d.	s. d.
-	-	-	10,413	[illegible]	[illegible]
-	-	3	[illegible]	[illegible]	[illegible]
-	1,000	-	71,819	1 10½	[illegible]
-	-	15	[illegible]	[illegible]	[illegible]
-	800	664	31,467	[illegible]	[illegible]
-	-	-	[illegible]	[illegible]	[illegible]
-	-	-	[illegible]	[illegible]	[illegible]
-	187	-	[illegible]	[illegible]	[illegible]
-	5,911	-	[illegible]	[illegible]	[illegible]
-	-	-	[illegible]	[illegible]	[illegible]
-	-	-	11,[illegible]	[illegible]	[illegible]
-	108	-	[illegible]	[illegible]	[illegible]
-	-	-	[illegible]	[illegible]	[illegible]
-	-	-	[illegible]	[illegible]	[illegible]
-	450	-	[illegible]	[illegible]	[illegible]
-	677	-	[illegible]	[illegible]	[illegible]
-	[illegible]	-	[illegible]	[illegible]	[illegible]
-	-	-	[illegible]	[illegible]	[illegible]
-	[illegible]	-	[illegible]	[illegible]	[illegible]
-	[illegible]	-	[illegible]	[illegible]	[illegible]
-	10	-	[illegible]	[illegible]	[illegible]
-	[illegible]	-	[illegible]	[illegible]	[illegible]
-	[illegible]	-	[illegible]	[illegible]	[illegible]
-	[illegible]	9	10,169	[illegible]	[illegible]
-	[illegible]	-	[illegible]	[illegible]	[illegible]
-	[illegible]	10	[illegible]	[illegible]	[illegible]
-	-	-	[illegible]	[illegible]	[illegible]
-	-	611	[illegible]	[illegible]	[illegible]
-	[illegible]	[illegible]	[illegible]	[illegible]	[illegible]
-	[illegible]	-	[illegible]	[illegible]	[illegible]
-	[illegible]	[illegible]	[illegible]	[illegible]	[illegible]
-	[illegible]	-	[illegible]	[illegible]	[illegible]
-	[illegible]	-	[illegible]	[illegible]	[illegible]
-	[illegible]	-	137,[illegible]	[illegible]	[illegible]
-	[illegible]	-	[illegible]	[illegible]	[illegible]
-	[illegible]	-	[illegible]	[illegible]	[illegible]
-	[illegible]	-	[illegible]	[illegible]	[illegible]
-	-	-	[illegible]	[illegible]	[illegible]
-	-	-	[illegible]	[illegible]	[illegible]
-	[illegible]	-	107,[illegible]	[illegible]	[illegible]
-	[illegible]	-	[illegible]	[illegible]	[illegible]
-	[illegible]	-	[illegible]	[illegible]	[illegible]
-	[illegible]	-	[illegible]	[illegible]	[illegible]
-	-	-	[illegible]	[illegible]	[illegible]
-	-	-	[illegible]	[illegible]	[illegible]
-	[illegible]	[illegible]	[illegible]	[illegible]	[illegible]

Part I.—Return showing the Receipts and Expenditure

Names of Counties and Unions.	Receipts.					Seed Rate Lodged.	Expenditure.			
	Amount of Poor Rate Lodged.	[illegible]	Other Receipts, [illegible]	Amount of Loans.	Total Receipts during the Year, [illegible]		In-Maintenance.	Out-Relief.	[illegible]	[illegible]
1.	2.	3.	4.	5.	6.	7.	8.	9.	10.	11.
PROVINCE OF LEINSTER.	£	£	£	£	£	£	£	£	£	£
Carlow.										
Carlow,	13,[illegible]	1,[illegible]	177	-	14,[illegible]	-	4,[illegible]	3,[illegible]	[illegible]	7
Dublin.										
Balrothery,	4,976	[illegible]	[illegible]	[illegible]	6,171	-	1,410	1,[illegible]	30	-
Dublin, North	45,115	8,[illegible]	4,816	1,570	64,[illegible]	-	74,[illegible]	4,317	761	[illegible]
Dublin, South,	60,[illegible]	8,141	1,[illegible]	-	62,[illegible]	-	[illegible]	5,[illegible]	8,[illegible]	[illegible]
Rathdown,	14,[illegible]	[illegible]	1,[illegible]	765	16,[illegible]	-	8,401	[illegible]	[illegible]	-
Kildare.										
Athy,	8,[illegible]	[illegible]	[illegible]	671	10,[illegible]	-	8,[illegible]	2,[illegible]	[illegible]	-
Celbridge,	6,[illegible]	170	19	400	7,[illegible]	-	1,[illegible]	1,814	[illegible]	-
Naas,	8,[illegible]	[illegible]	384	3,441	14,361	-	2,[illegible]	2,[illegible]	[illegible]	7
Kilkenny.										
Callan,	8,[illegible]	[illegible]	44	1,165	9,[illegible]	-	2,[illegible]	1,[illegible]	[illegible]	[illegible]
Castlecomer,	4,187	[illegible]	45	[illegible]	4,[illegible]	-	1,[illegible]	[illegible]	7	[illegible]
Kilkenny,	8,[illegible]	[illegible]	194	-	11,[illegible]	-	6,[illegible]	2,[illegible]	[illegible]	[illegible]
Thomastown,	4,[illegible]	[illegible]	[illegible]	[illegible]	6,074	-	1,[illegible]	1,[illegible]	34	-
Urlingford,	8,[illegible]	210	[illegible]	-	3,[illegible]	-	1,[illegible]	[illegible]	[illegible]	-
King's Co.										
Edenderry,	4,[illegible]	[illegible]	9	-	5,142	-	1,410	[illegible]	[illegible]	-
Parsonstown,	4,913	[illegible]	152	-	5,[illegible]	-	1,761	319	[illegible]	[illegible]
Tullamore,	6,[illegible]	[illegible]	1[illegible]	4,[illegible]	11,[illegible]	-	[illegible]	7,[illegible]	[illegible]	[illegible]
Longford.										
Ballymahon,	4,[illegible]	[illegible]	19	3,814	8,[illegible]	-	1,274	[illegible]	[illegible]	[illegible]
Granard,	6,[illegible]	879	[illegible]	-	6,[illegible]	-	1,[illegible]	2,[illegible]	[illegible]	[illegible]
Longford,	6,714	431	1[illegible]	[illegible]	8,[illegible]	51	[illegible]	1,[illegible]	71	-
Louth.										
Ardee,	6,219	477	[illegible]	-	6,[illegible]	-	1,701	1,[illegible]	[illegible]	-
Drogheda,	10,[illegible]	[illegible]	167	4,404	15,[illegible]	-	3,[illegible]	3,216	[illegible]	-
Dundalk,	9,157	[illegible]	145	[illegible]	10,[illegible]	-	9,[illegible]	2,[illegible]	179	-
Meath.										
Dunshaughlin,	4,[illegible]	[illegible]	279	1,[illegible]	6,[illegible]	-	1,[illegible]	1,047	[illegible]	-
Kells,	8,[illegible]	[illegible]	[illegible]	4,[illegible]	13,[illegible]	-	2,[illegible]	2,147	[illegible]	-
Navan,	6,[illegible]	[illegible]	[illegible]	6,[illegible]	15,[illegible]	-	[illegible]	2,[illegible]	[illegible]	1
Oldcastle,	[illegible]	915	4	2,[illegible]	7,[illegible]	1	1,[illegible]	[illegible]	[illegible]	[illegible]
Trim,	6,[illegible]	[illegible]	[illegible]	2,[illegible]	11,164	-	1,797	[illegible]	77	-
Queen's Co.										
Abbeyleix,	6,[illegible]	[illegible]	[illegible]	-	6,[illegible]	-	1,[illegible]	1,[illegible]	45	-
Mountmellick,	8,[illegible]	[illegible]	[illegible]	-	7,[illegible]	-	2,[illegible]	2,[illegible]	[illegible]	-
Westmeath.										
Athlone,	4,[illegible]	[illegible]	172	-	[illegible]	-	2,161	1,[illegible]	[illegible]	[illegible]
Delvin,	3,[illegible]	[illegible]	[illegible]	4,[illegible]	[illegible]	-	915	776	[illegible]	-
Mullingar,	12,[illegible]	[illegible]	[illegible]	6,[illegible]	18,[illegible]	-	2,[illegible]	3,[illegible]	[illegible]	[illegible]
Wexford.										
Enniscorthy,	7,[illegible]	[illegible]	[illegible]	2,[illegible]	10,[illegible]	-	[illegible]	[illegible]	[illegible]	-
Gorey,	6,[illegible]	316	[illegible]	[illegible]	9,[illegible]	-	7,[illegible]	[illegible]	[illegible]	-
New Ross,	8,[illegible]	[illegible]	90	[illegible]	9,[illegible]	-	4,184	[illegible]	[illegible]	-
Wexford,	[illegible]	[illegible]	[illegible]	6,[illegible]	15,[illegible]	-	3,[illegible]	1,[illegible]	[illegible]	-
Wicklow.										
Baltinglass,	[illegible]	707	41	[illegible]	6,[illegible]	-	1,071	1,181	15	[illegible]
Rathdrum,	7,[illegible]	[illegible]	[illegible]	[illegible]	[illegible]	-	2,[illegible]	2,[illegible]	[illegible]	-
Shillelagh,	[illegible]	[illegible]	[illegible]	-	6,[illegible]	-	1,[illegible]	[illegible]	[illegible]	-
Total, Leinster, } [illegible]	[illegible]	95,[illegible]	14,[illegible]	[illegible]	410,[illegible]	[illegible]	134,[illegible]	73,[illegible]	4,[illegible]	[illegible]
Total, Leinster, } [illegible]	[illegible]	[illegible]	16,[illegible]	[illegible]	434,[illegible]	1,[illegible]	143,[illegible]	73,[illegible]	[illegible]	[illegible]
Increase,	-	-	-	14,[illegible]	-	-	-	[illegible]	1,[illegible]	[illegible]
Decrease,	11,[illegible]	1,[illegible]	[illegible]	-	[illegible]	1,[illegible]	8,797	-	-	-

Year ended 29th September, 1887—*continued.*

Expenditure—							continued.	
[illegible]	[illegible]	Expenses under the Public Health Acts.		[illegible]	[illegible]	[illegible]	[illegible]	Names of Counties and Unions.
		For Sanitary purposes.	For Burial Grounds.					
15.	16.	17.	18.	19.	20.	21.	22.	23.
£	£	£	£	£	£	£	£	PROVINCE OF LEINSTER. CARLOW.
1,732	63	464	–	48	1,416	181	–	Carlow.

PART I.—RETURN showing the Receipts and Expenditure of Unions during the Year ended 29th September, 1887—*continued.*

Names of Counties and Unions.	Expenditure—(continued).			Amount of Expenditure included in Columns 15 and 27 defrayed out of Loans.		[illegible]	Valuation on 29th Sept., 1887.	Poundage on the Valuation.	
	[illegible]	Repayment of Loans.	[illegible]	Poor Relief.	Other Expenditure.			[illegible]	[illegible]
24.	25.	26.	27.	28.	29.	30.	31.	32.	33.
PROVINCE OF LEINSTER.	£	£	£	£	£	£	£	s. d.	s. d.
CARLOW.									
Carlow,	237	–	16,180	–	–	–	150,190	1 4½	2 6½
DUBLIN.									
Balrothery,	244	38	7,604	–	242	–	84,795	0 8	1 8
Dublin, North,	332	1,970	54,772	–	1,896	–	389,817	2 0½	2 9½
Dublin, South,	1,214	1,640	63,778	–	–	–	607,892	1 4½	1 9
Rathdown,	480	418	25,188	–	776	–	270,740	0 10	1 9
KILDARE.									
Athy,	176	44	10,251	–	382	–	111,604	1 6½	1 10
Celbridge,	101	–	7,794	–	400	–	111,531	0 11	1 2½
Naas,	125	60	11,083	–	1,481	–	138,188	1 0½	1 6½
KILKENNY.									
Callan,	101	130	7,435	–	119	–	78,378	1 7½	2 4½
Castlecomer,	94	62	4,807	–	18	–	73,097	0 9	1 4½
Kilkenny,	191	–	10,960	–	–	–	80,734	1 7½	2 2
Thomastown,	107	30	5,376	–	120	–	70,140	1 1	1 6
Urlingford,	70	48	3,811	–	–	–	65,793	1 2	1 4½
KING'S CO.									
Edenderry,	148	63	9,488	–	–	–	95,645	0 9½	1 8
Parsonstown,	163	17	8,873	–	–	–	103,779	0 9½	1 5
Tullamore,	170	–	12,980	–	4,333	–	141,267	1 7½	1 9½
LONGFORD.									
Ballymahon,	89	–	7,095	–	3,720	–	61,490	1 6½	1 9
Granard,	146	36	8,530	–	–	–	85,482	1 2½	1 7½
Longford,	124	89	6,785	–	331	31	60,673	1 1	1 11½
LOUTH.									
Ardee,	63	157	6,413	–	27	–	64,471	0 11½	1 [illegible]
Drogheda,	180	304	11,033	–	2,600	–	103,103	1 2	1 11
Dundalk,	240	10	10,306	–	360	–	102,917	1 4½	1 8½
MEATH.									
Dunshaughlin,	125	84	7,083	–	500	–	100,796	0 11	1 4½
Kells,	111	170	12,567	–	3,011	–	80,674	1 4	2 6½
Navan,	251	243	15,114	–	6,011	–	84,160	1 0½	2 1½
Oldcastle,	25	–	6,210	–	1,571	13	62,701	1 1½	1 8½
Trim,	104	117	4,460	–	–	–	109,304	1 2	1 4½
QUEEN'S CO.									
Abbeyleix,	123	60	6,394	–	–	–	90,870	1 4½	1 6
Mountmellick,	101	113	8,800	–	–	–	102,095	1 1½	1 9
WESTMEATH.									
Athlone,	84	88	8,987	–	–	–	97,750	1 1	1 6½
Delvin,	60	378	8,488	–	4,418	–	69,008	1 0½	2 4½
Mullingar,	318	397	10,330	–	2,330	–	146,417	1 0½	1 8½
WEXFORD.									
Enniscorthy,	327	374	11,781	–	2,297	–	111,891	1 4½	1 9½
Gorey,	127	60	8,103	–	480	–	90,451	0 10	1 6½
New Ross,	139	–	11,899	–	–	–	104,488	1 4½	1 10½
Wexford,	138	248	12,088	–	3,755	–	105,320	1 4½	1 9½
WICKLOW.									
Baltinglass,	71	86	8,401	–	797	–	73,770	1 10	1 8
Rathdrum,	115	186	9,081	–	780	–	109,411	1 0	1 8
Shillelagh,	126	–	1,144	–	–	–	50,921	1 4½	1 7½
Total, Leinster, 1887,	6,646	7,709	483,484	–	42,974	67	4,798,617	1 3½	1 10
Total, Leinster, 1886,	6,719	5,480	486,305	–	55,406	3,553	4,781,470	1 4½	1 9
Increase,	1,925	2,216	–	–	–	–	–	–	0 0½
Decrease,	–	–	2,884	–	12,532	3,486	18,804	0 0½	–

PART I.—RETURN showing the Receipts and Expenditure of Unions during the Year ended 29th September, 1887—*continued.*

Name of Counties and Unions.	Receipts.					Seed Rate Lodged.	Expenditure—(continued).			
	Amount of Poor Rate Lodged.	Parliamentary Grants.	Other Receipts, including repayments of Relief by way of Loan, &c.	Amount of Loans.	Total Receipts during the Year, exclusive of Seed Rate.		In-Maintenance.	Out-Relief.	[illegible]	Vaccination Expenses.
1.	2.	3.	4.	5.	6.	7.	8.	9.	10.	11.
PROVINCE OF CONNAUGHT.	£	£	£	£	£	£	£	£	£	£
Galway.										
Ballinasloe,	6,461	689	37	-	7,476	66	6,476	488	90	15
Clifden,	3,479	470	67	-	4,083	6	824	731	-	-
Galway,	6,975	617	476	-	8,077	80	2,580	647	51	9
Glennamaddy,	2,971	584	16	-	3,563	51	978	683	22	-
Gort,	3,411	388	94	-	3,893	4	1,496	668	75	61
Loughrea,	4,081	398	82	-	4,559	8	1,316	1,098	67	10
Mountbellew,	2,475	322	13	-	2,787	5	973	987	13	91
Oughterard,	2,733	325	1,438	-	4,391	-	715	361	38	-
Portumna,	2,035	784	59	-	2,878	-	1,779	483	-	-
Tuam,	6,567	718	79	-	7,313	14	1,676	1,318	73	-
Leitrim.										
Carrick-on-Shannon,	1,708	449	49	-	2,205	-	1,763	1,076	76	46
Manorhamilton,	2,379	816	3	88	3,287	-	1,135	486	84	-
Mohill,	3,833	340	18	-	4,191	13	1,452	689	34	8
Mayo.										
Ballina,	4,642	654	169	-	6,188	609	1,400	874	63	4
Ballinrobe,	4,585	666	37	-	5,188	-	1,497	690	33	-
Belmullet,	1,843	866	454	-	2,757	-	677	57	6	396
Castlebar,	2,897	573	85	-	3,305	6	461	238	101	-
Claremorris,	3,838	525	4	-	4,348	-	880	976	67	43
Killala,	2,443	611	33	-	2,882	-	882	875	-	-
Swinford,	5,888	807	180	66	7,380	833	1,368	808	891	-
Westport,	5,388	653	133	-	6,087	6	3,149	836	108	4
Roscommon.										
Boyle,	8,511	783	67	305	9,348	112	1,467	1,337	89	41
Castlerea,	4,781	908	19	1,088	6,975	9	1,843	753	83	13
Roscommon,	6,827	781	114	-	6,847	43	2,335	888	68	77
Strokestown,	5,195	443	41	-	5,649	11	1,169	1,103	60	10
Sligo.										
Dromore West,	2,627	383	64	-	3,074	33	617	880	17	7
Sligo,	7,034	367	154	-	8,545	150	8,267	1,103	62	-
Tobercurry,	1,718	468	31	1,241	3,461	60	663	1,190	95	-
Total, Connaught, 1887,	130,149	13,767	(a) [illegible]	[illegible]	130,417	1,839	37,036	21,083	1,304	753
Total, Connaught, 1886,	124,621	13,710	(b) 20,731	4,631	144,903	2,248	34,966	55,[illegible]	1,324	780
Increase,	4,550	-	-	-	-	-	-	-	-	-
Decrease,	-	480	16,843	1,381	14,486	[illegible]	1,730	34,[illegible]	10	9
SUMMARY OF PROVINCES.										
Ulster,	710,800	83,921	3,871	2,189	817,784	736	66,118	84,685	8,378	83
Munster,	356,[illegible]	26,988	7,118	83,080	473,762	390	153,151	88,306	4,274	734
Leinster,	351,[illegible]	86,368	14,330	64,418	516,[illegible]	35	186,811	73,171	4,994	949
Connaught,	130,185	19,769	3,679	8,080	160,427	1,839	37,036	81,083	1,304	753
Total, Ireland, 1887,	1,538,878	88,884	28,[illegible]	158,[illegible]	1,910,461	3,635	376,[illegible]	307,130	13,7[illegible]	1,158
Total, Ireland, 1886,	1,537,[illegible]	93,[illegible]	49,813	191,971	1,[illegible]	15,836	383,194	335,[illegible]	13,408	1,017
Increase,	1,350	-	-	37,[illegible]	6,485	-	-	-	307	341
Decrease,	-	4,6[illegible]	[illegible]	-	-	13,241	12,[illegible]	[illegible],076	-	-

(a) Includes a sum of £1,631, and (b) a sum of £18,372 being the portion of the Grant of £20,000 under the Poor Relief Act, 1886, brought into the Union accounts for the years ended 29th September, 1887 and 1886, respectively.

[*continued.*

Return of the Receipts

of Unions during the Year ended 29th September, 1887—*continued.*

Expenditure.			Amount of Expenditure included in Columns [illegible] defrayed out of Loans.		[illegible]	Valuation for 29th Sept., 1887.	Poundage on Net Valuation.		Names of Counties and Unions.
Expenses under the Parliamentary Voters, Jurors, and Registration Acts.	Repayment of Loans.	Total Expenditure [illegible]	Poor Relief.	Other Expenditure.			[illegible]	[illegible]	
34.	35.	36.	37.	38.	39.	40.	41.	42.	43.
									PROVINCE OF CONNAUGHT.
£	£	£	£	£	£	£	s. d.	s. d.	GALWAY.
131	103	6,446	-	-	63	78,093	1 3½	1 8	Ballinasloe.
76	91	3,731	-	-	-	17,498	3 0½	4 6½	Clifden.
163	401	8,624	-	-	48	85,680	1 8½	2 1½	Galway.
79	61	5,072	-	-	40	51,388	1 4½	1 11½	Glennamaddy.
64	64	4,801	-	-	-	43,115	1 8½	2 0	Gort.
148	280	6,380	-	148	9	78,806	0 11½	1 4½	Loughrea.
41	-	3,380	-	-	6	40,410	1 0½	1 8½	Mountbellew.
150	-	3,993	-	-	300	14,394	3 1½	4 1½	Oughterard.
9	74	3,316	-	-	-	36,883	1 4½	1 9½	Portumna.
178	71	7,379	-	-	23	76,830	1 4½	1 11	Tuam.
									LEITRIM.
140	84	6,738	-	-	-	48,880	1 6	2 2	Car.-on-Shannon.
61	87	3,868	-	-	-	48,430	1 8	1 9½	Manorhamilton.
88	58	4,806	-	-	17	39,489	1 9½	2 4½	Mohill.
									MAYO.
88	79	4,486	-	-	1,270	49,470	1 4½	2 0½	Ballina.
184	76	6,123	-	-	-	60,173	1 8	2 3½	Ballinrobe.
88	63	3,337	-	-	249	10,985	2 10½	4 7	Belmullet.
91	-	5,415	-	-	2	46,154	1 0	1 6½	Castlebar.
83	87	4,111	-	64	436	42,481	1 8½	1 11	Claremorris.
47	-	2,159	-	-	809	30,908	1 8	2 1½	Killala.
194	204	4,347	-	107	2,748	40,380	1 11	2 11½	Swinford.
86	39	4,819	-	-	-	44,380	1 4½	2 2½	Westport.
									ROSCOMMON.
168	79	6,681	-	104	88	71,186	1 9½	1 9½	Boyle.
67	263	3,794	-	1,477	11	78,018	0 11½	1 8½	Castlerea.
88	52	5,763	-	-	19	64,487	1 8	1 6½	Roscommon.
63	646	4,011	-	-	-	60,609	1 6	1 11½	Strokestown.
									SLIGO.
182	80	2,951	-	-	45	38,946	0 11½	1 7½	Dromore West.
279	308	7,725	-	-	45	89,376	1 0½	1 6½	Sligo.
23	78	6,694	-	1,510	2,421	40,764	1 8½	2 9½	Tobercurry.
2,805	4,505	184,063	-	3,275	6,216	1,306,429	1 4½	1 11½	1887, Total,
1,754	3,877	176,611	-	2,841	73,395	1,306,358	1 4½	2 2½	1886, Connaught.
1,051	-	-	-	434	-	71	-	-	Increase.
-	676	37,588	-	-	16,719	-	0 4	0 3½	Decrease.

PROVINCES.

34.	35.	36.	37.	38.	39.	40.	41.	42.	43.
6,980	8,130	843,213	60	7,781	399	4,068,031	0 6½	1 1½	ULSTER.
8,448	19,030	498,835	-	78,116	8,180	3,411,270	1 0½	2 8	MUNSTER.
5,946	7,788	463,431	-	42,874	87	4,748,343	1 8½	1 9½	LEINSTER.
2,805	8,507	184,063	-	3,325	6,278	1,306,429	1 4½	1 11½	CONNAUGHT.
23,668	43,469	1,138,704	60	180,008	9,211	13,617,088	1 7½	1 9½	1887, TOTAL,
16,668	38,441	1,160,097	-	136,311	33,189	13,598,770	1 2½	1 9½	1886, IRELAND.
7,003	5,094	-	60	-	-	18,318	-	-	Increase.
-	-	21,393	-	7,303	24,778	-	0 0½	-	Decrease.

of Ba'gmullet and [illegible] Unions, respectively; expenditure to the amount of the former having been defrayed [from] the balance of the Grant made under the Poor Relief Act, 1880.

[illegible]

[illegible]	[illegible]				[illegible]	[illegible]	[illegible]	[illegible]			[illegible]		
	[illegible]	[illegible]	[illegible]	[illegible]				[illegible]	[illegible]	[illegible]	[illegible]	[illegible]	[illegible]
[illegible]								£	£	£	s. d.	s. d.	s. d.
[illegible]													
[illegible]	[illegible]	[illegible]	[illegible]	[illegible]	[illegible]	[illegible]	[illegible]	[illegible]	[illegible]	[illegible]	[illegible]	[illegible]	[illegible]
[illegible]													
[illegible]	[illegible]	[illegible]	[illegible]	[illegible]	[illegible]	[illegible]	[illegible]	[illegible]	[illegible]	[illegible]	[illegible]	[illegible]	[illegible]

[illegible]	[illegible]	[illegible]	[illegible]	[illegible]	[illegible]	[illegible]	[illegible]	[illegible]	[illegible]	[illegible]
[illegible]	[illegible]	[illegible]	[illegible]	[illegible]	[illegible]	[illegible]	[illegible]	[illegible]	[illegible]	[illegible]
[illegible]	[illegible]	[illegible]	[illegible]	[illegible]	[illegible]	[illegible]	[illegible]	[illegible]	[illegible]	[illegible]
[illegible]	[illegible]	[illegible]	[illegible]	[illegible]	[illegible]	[illegible]	[illegible]	[illegible]	[illegible]	[illegible]

SUMMARY OF PROVINCES.

[illegible]	[illegible]	[illegible]	[illegible]	[illegible]	[illegible]	[illegible]	[illegible]	[illegible]	[illegible]	[illegible]
[illegible]	[illegible]	[illegible]	[illegible]	[illegible]	[illegible]	[illegible]	[illegible]	[illegible]	[illegible]	[illegible]
[illegible]	[illegible]	[illegible]	[illegible]	[illegible]	[illegible]	[illegible]	[illegible]	[illegible]	[illegible]	[illegible]
[illegible]	[illegible]	[illegible]	[illegible]	[illegible]	[illegible]	[illegible]	[illegible]	[illegible]	[illegible]	[illegible]
[illegible]	[illegible]	[illegible]	[illegible]	[illegible]	[illegible]	[illegible]	[illegible]	[illegible]	[illegible]	[illegible]
[illegible]	[illegible]	[illegible]	[illegible]	[illegible]	[illegible]	[illegible]	[illegible]	[illegible]	[illegible]	[illegible]

No. 2.—Classification of Persons Relieved in Union Workhouses in Ireland, during each of the Half-years ended 25th March and 29th September, 1887, respectively.

	Classes of Persons Relieved in Workhouses.	No. in the Half-year ended 25th March, 1887.	No. in the Half-year ended 29th September, 1887.
	ABLE-BODIED AND THEIR CHILDREN.		
1	Adults, Married Couples, Males,	6,617	7,187
2	Adults, Married Couples, Females,	6,617	7,187
3	Adults, Other Males,	78,585	65,094
4	Adults, Other Females,	26,130	31,616
5	Children under 15, of Able-bodied Inmates, Illegitimate,	5,053	6,505
6	Children under 15, of Able-bodied Inmates, Other Children,	20,737	23,683
	NOT ABLE-BODIED.		
7	Adults, Married Couples, Males,	629	697
8	Adults, Married Couples, Females,	629	697
9	Adults, Other Males,	27,106	30,284
10	Adults, Other Females,	17,989	19,981
11	Children under 15, Of Parents not able-bodied being Inmates, Illegitimate,	460	545
12	Children under 15, Of Parents not able-bodied being Inmates, Other Children,	1,501	1,973
13	Children under 15, Orphans, or other Children relieved without Parents,	6,773	7,301
	LUNATICS, INSANE PERSONS, AND IDIOTS.		
14	Adult Males,	1,583	1,563
15	Adult Females,	2,187	2,169
16	Children under 15,	102	84
17	Total number of Males,	115,716	128,271
18	Do. Females,	35,749	87,743
19	Do. Children under 15,	53,008	42,308
20	Grand Total,	204,773	250,383

No. 8.—Classification of Persons Relieved out of the Workhouses in Unions in Ireland, during each of the Half-years ended 25th March and 29th September, 1887, respectively, including Persons relieved in Blind and Deaf and Dumb Asylums.

No.	Classes of Persons Relieved.	Number in the Half-year ended 25th March, 1887.	Number in the Half-year ended 29th Sept., 1887.
1	Blind Persons maintained in Asylums, Males,	132	146
2	Blind Persons maintained in Asylums, Females,	223	236
3	Deaf and Dumb Persons maintained in Asylums, Males,	234	237
4	Deaf and Dumb Persons maintained in Asylums, Females,	204	200
	Total,	813	839
	RELIEVED UNDER 10 VIC., c. 31, SEC. 1.		
5	Adult Males permanently disabled by old age or infirmity,	10,110	10,426
6	Families of Adult Males under heading 5, Wives,	5,103	5,278
7	Families of Adult Males under heading 5, Children under 15,	2,235	2,467
8	Adult Males relieved in cases of their own sickness or accident,	7,096	6,690
9	Families of Adult Males under heading 8, Wives,	5,436	5,177
10	Families of Adult Males under heading 8, Children under 15,	13,366	14,733
11	Adult Women permanently disabled by old age or infirmity,	21,109	23,241
12	Children under 15, of Women under heading 11, Legitimate,	328	493
13	Children under 15, of Women under heading 11, Illegitimate,	37	84
14	Adult Women relieved in cases of sickness or accident,	4,151	4,350
15	Children under 15, of Women under heading 14, Legitimate,	2,103	2,437
16	Children under 15, of Women under heading 14, Illegitimate,	113	103
17	Able-bodied Widows, having two or more legitimate children dependent on them,	4,176	4,434
18	Children under 15, dependent on Widows under heading 17,	13,806	14,683
19	Lunatics, Insane Persons, and Idiots, Males,	93	90
20	Lunatics, Insane Persons, and Idiots, Females,	73	81
21	Lunatics, Insane Persons, and Idiots, Children under 15,	59	56
	Total,	89,562	96,843
	PERSONS RELIEVED UNDER 10 VIC., c. 31, BUT NOT UNDER SEC. 1.		
22	Adult Males, married or single, relieved on account of want of work,	–	–
23	Families of Adult Males under heading 22, Wives,	–	–
24	Families of Adult Males under heading 22, Children under 15,	–	–
25	Able-bodied Women, Unmarried,	–	–
26	Able-bodied Women, Widows not relievable under sec. 1,	–	–
27	Children of Women under headings 25 and 26, Legitimate,	–	–
28	Children of Women under headings 25 and 26, Illegitimate,	–	–
	Families Relieved without Husband or Father.		
29	Husband or Father in Gaol, Wives,	–	–
30	Husband or Father in Gaol, Children under 15,	–	–
31	Husband or Father on service in Army or Navy, Wives,	–	–
32	Husband or Father on service in Army or Navy, Children under 15,	–	–
33	Deserted by Husband or Father, Wives,	–	–
34	Deserted by Husband or Father, Children under 15,	–	–
35	Orphans and children relieved without either parent,	–	–
36	Number of persons relieved provisionally, and not included in the foregoing,	4,706	5,038
	Total,	4,706	5,038
37	Number of persons relieved under 11 & 12 Vic., c. 47, sec. 4, and not included in the foregoing,	796	841
38	Orphans or Deserted Children out at Nurse under 39 and 40 Vic., sec. 38,	2,759	2,801
	Grand Total (Nos. 5 to 38 inclusive),	97,823	105,523

No. 4.—Summary of Returns from Clerks of Unions, showing for each Province, and for all Ireland, the Number of Persons admitted to the Workhouses during the Year ended 29th September, 1887, distinguishing the Number admitted in Sickness; also the Number of Births and Deaths in the Workhouses during the Year.

Provinces.	Number of Persons admitted during the Year.						No. of Births in the Workhouses during the Year.	No. of Deaths in the Workhouses during the Year.
	Number admitted in Sickness.				Number admitted who were not sick.	Total number admitted during the Year.		
	Suffering under Fever or other dangerous contagious disease.	Suffering under other disease.	Suffering from accidental injury.	Total number admitted in sickness.				
Ulster, . .	813	6,730	554	8,187	58,470	66,657	648	1,165
Munster, . .	1,476	16,711	1,021	19,189	93,904	112,173	430	2,575
Leinster, . .	1,517	17,048	673	19,238	117,784	136,142	847	3,444
Connaught, . .	413	3,370	531	4,381	22,657	26,948	80	936
Total, Ireland,	4,218	44,879	2,829	51,024	291,840	343,860	1,183	10,120

No. 5.—Summary of Returns showing for each Province, and for all Ireland, the Number of Sick Persons who received Medical treatment in the Workhouse Hospitals and Fever Hospitals, during the Year ended 29th September, 1887.

Provinces.	Under treatment at the commencement of the Year.				New Cases.				Total Cases treated in Hospitals during the Year.			
	Fever or other dangerous contagious disease.	Other diseases.	Accidentally injured.	Total.	Fever or other dangerous contagious disease.	Other diseases.	Accidentally injured.	Total.	Fever or other dangerous contagious disease.	Other diseases.	Accidentally injured.	Total.
Ulster, . .	113	2,867	73	3,037	1,330	16,057	677	18,072	1,441	18,921	837	20,[illegible]
Munster, . .	125	4,1[illegible]	120	4,438	1,[illegible]35	26,031	1,214	28,770	9,0[illegible]	27,[illegible]53	1,330	33,135
Leinster, . .	140	2,920	143	3,218	2,00[illegible]	32,514	1,130	35,411	2,2[illegible]	31,141	1,330	37,632
Connaught, . .	55	1,434	67	1,577	619	5,143	287	6,128	674	6,648	436	7,718
Total, Ireland,	433	12,452	413	13,337	6,321	72,171	3,540	81,034	6,816	87,037	4,033	98,[illegible]

[illegible]—Statement (in pursuance of Sec. 20 of 12 & 13 Vic., c. 104) relative to the Audit of Union Accounts [illegible] of Statement in Fifteenth Annual Report of the Local Government Board (Ireland), 1887, Appendix D, No. 6.

I. Date up to which the Accounts of Unions have been audited.

The Accounts of all the Unions have been audited up to the 29th September, 1887, excepting those of [illegible] Union.

II. Sums disallowed or found due on Audit of the Accounts of Unions in Ireland, up to 29th September, 1887, and whether recovered or in course of recovery from the Parties liable.

Union.	Half-year ended	Date of Audit.	Amount disallowed or found due.	Whether paid or in course of recovery.	Observations—Personal items disallowed, &c.
			£ s. d.		
[illegible]	[illegible] March, 1887,	[illegible], 1887,	[illegible]	Paid.	[illegible]
"	[illegible] Sept., 1887,	[illegible], 1887,	[illegible]	Paid.	[illegible]
"	"	—	[illegible]	Not enforced.	[illegible]
[illegible]	[illegible] March, 1887,	[illegible], 1887,	[illegible]	Paid.	[illegible]
"	[illegible] Sept., 1887,	[illegible], 1888,	[illegible]	In course of recovery.	[illegible]
[illegible]		[illegible], 1887,	[illegible]	Paid.	[illegible]
[illegible]	[illegible] March, 1887,	[illegible], 1887,	[illegible]	Paid.	[illegible]
[illegible]			[illegible]	In course of recovery.	[illegible]
[illegible]	[illegible] Sept., 1887,	[illegible] March, 1888,	[illegible]	In course of recovery.	[illegible]
[illegible]	"	[illegible] Nov., 1887,	[illegible]	Paid.	[illegible]
"	"	"	[illegible]	Not enforced.	[illegible]

No. 6.—[illegible] (in pursuance of Sec. [illegible] of 12 and 13 Vic., c. 104) relative to the [illegible] [illegible] of [illegible] Local Government Board (Ireland), 18[illegible], Appendix [illegible], No. [illegible])—continued.

[illegible] [illegible] Audits of the Accounts of Unions in Ireland, up to [illegible] September, 18[illegible], and whether [illegible] [illegible] [illegible].

[illegible]	[illegible]	[illegible]	[illegible]	[illegible]	[illegible]
			£ s. d.		
[illegible]	[illegible]	[illegible]	[illegible]	Not paid,	[illegible]
"	"	"	[illegible]	Paid,	[illegible]
"	"	"	[illegible]	Not paid,	[illegible]
"	[illegible]	[illegible]	[illegible]	Not yet paid,	[illegible]
"	"	"	[illegible]	Not yet paid,	[illegible]
[illegible]	[illegible]	[illegible]	[illegible]	Paid,	[illegible]
[illegible]	[illegible]	[illegible]	[illegible]	Paid,	[illegible]
[illegible]	"	[illegible]	[illegible]	Not collected,	[illegible]
[illegible]	[illegible]	[illegible]	[illegible]	Not collected,	[illegible]
[illegible]	[illegible]	[illegible]	[illegible]	In course of recovery,	[illegible]
[illegible]	"	[illegible]	[illegible]	Proceedings deferred,	[illegible]
[illegible]	[illegible]	[illegible]	[illegible]	In course of recovery,	[illegible]
"	"	"	[illegible]	[illegible]	[illegible]
[illegible]		[illegible]	[illegible]	[illegible]	[illegible]
[illegible]	[illegible]	[illegible]	[illegible]	Paid,	[illegible]
[illegible]	"	[illegible]	[illegible]	Not collected,	[illegible]
[illegible]	[illegible]	[illegible]	[illegible]	Paid,	[illegible]
"	"	"	[illegible]	Paid,	[illegible]

No. 3.—Statement (in pursuance of Sec. [illegible] of 12 and 13 Vic., c. 104) relative to the Audit of Union Accounts;—in continuation of statement in Fifteenth Annual Report of the Local Government Board (Ireland), 1887, Appendix D., No. [illegible]—continued.

II. Sums [illegible] due on Audit of the Accounts of Unions in Ireland, up to 29th September, 1887, and whether [illegible] from the parties [illegible]—continued.

Union.	[illegible]	Date of Audit.	Amount [illegible]	Whether paid or [illegible]	Observations—[illegible]
			£ s. d.		
[illegible]	[illegible] March, 1887.	[illegible] July, 1887.	[illegible]	Paid.	[illegible]
[illegible]	[illegible]	[illegible] 1887.	[illegible]	Not collected.	[illegible]
[illegible]	[illegible]	[illegible] 1887.	[illegible]	Paid.	[illegible]
[illegible]	[illegible]	[illegible]	[illegible]	Not collected.	[illegible]
[illegible]	[illegible] Sept., 1886.	11 Feb., 1887.	[illegible]	[illegible]	[illegible]
[illegible]	[illegible] March, 1887.	[illegible] July, 1887.	[illegible]	Paid.	[illegible]
[illegible]	[illegible] Sept., 1887.	[illegible] 1887.	[illegible]	Paid.	[illegible]
[illegible]	[illegible] March, 1887.	[illegible] 1887.	[illegible]	Not paid.	[illegible]
[illegible]	[illegible] Sept., 1887.	[illegible] Nov., 1887.	[illegible]	Not collected.	[illegible]
[illegible]	[illegible]	[illegible] Dec., 1887.	[illegible]	Paid.	[illegible]
[illegible]	[illegible]	[illegible]	[illegible]	Not paid.	[illegible]

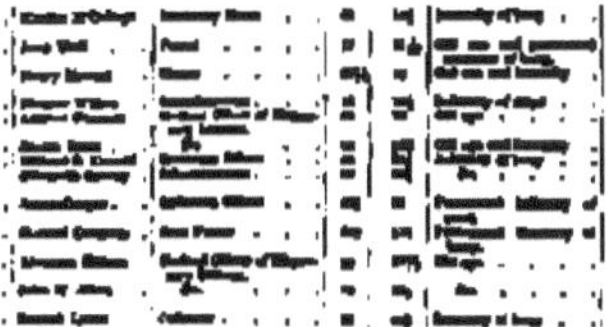

[illegible]	Infirmity of body	[illegible]	[illegible]
[illegible]	Old age	[illegible]	[illegible]
[illegible]	Permanent infirmity of body	[illegible]	[illegible]
[illegible]	Infirmity of mind and body	[illegible]	[illegible]
[illegible]	Old age	[illegible]	[illegible]
[illegible]	Infirmity of body	[illegible]	[illegible]
[illegible]	Do.	[illegible]	[illegible]
[illegible]	Do.	[illegible]	[illegible]
[illegible]	Infirmity of mind and body	[illegible]	[illegible]
[illegible]	Permanent infirmity of body	[illegible]	[illegible]
[illegible]	Old age	[illegible]	[illegible]
[illegible]	Infirmity of mind and body	[illegible]	[illegible]
[illegible]	Permanent infirmity of mind and body	[illegible]	[illegible]
[illegible]	Old age and permanent infirmity of body	[illegible]	[illegible]
[illegible]	Do.	[illegible]	[illegible]
[illegible]	Permanent [illegible] of mind	[illegible]	[illegible]
[illegible]	[illegible]	[illegible]	[illegible]
[illegible]	Infirmity of body	[illegible]	[illegible]
[illegible]	Do.	[illegible]	[illegible]
[illegible]	Permanent infirmity of body	[illegible]	[illegible]
[illegible]	Permanent infirmity of mind	[illegible]	[illegible]
[illegible]	Infirmity of body	[illegible]	[illegible]
[illegible]	Old age	[illegible]	[illegible]
[illegible]	Old age and [illegible]	[illegible]	[illegible]
[illegible]	Do.	[illegible]	[illegible]
[illegible]	Permanent infirmity of body	[illegible]	[illegible]

No. 7.—Union Officers' Superannuation.—Statement of Allowances under the Superannuation Acts in force during any portion of the year ended [illegible] September, 18[illegible]; showing also the cases in which the Allowances had terminated during the Year. (In continuation of Statement in the [illegible] Report of the Local Government Board (Ireland), 18[illegible], Appendix D, No. [illegible])—continued.

[illegible]	Union.	Name of Officer.	Office.	Age.	[illegible]	[illegible]	[illegible]	[illegible]	[illegible]
							£ s. d.	£ s. d.	
[illegible]	[illegible]	[illegible]	[illegible]	[illegible]	[illegible]	[illegible]	[illegible]	[illegible]	
[illegible]	Do.	[illegible]	[illegible]	[illegible]	[illegible]	[illegible]	[illegible]	[illegible]	
[illegible]	[illegible]	[illegible]	[illegible]	[illegible]	[illegible]	[illegible]	[illegible]	[illegible]	
[illegible]	Do.	[illegible]	[illegible]	[illegible]	[illegible]	[illegible]	[illegible]	[illegible]	[illegible]
[illegible]	Do.	[illegible]	[illegible]	[illegible]	[illegible]	[illegible]	[illegible]	[illegible]	
[illegible]	Do.	[illegible]	[illegible]	[illegible]	[illegible]	[illegible]	[illegible]	[illegible]	
[illegible]	[illegible]	[illegible]	[illegible]	[illegible]	[illegible]	[illegible]	[illegible]	[illegible]	
[illegible]	Do.	[illegible]	[illegible]	[illegible]	[illegible]	Do.	[illegible]	[illegible]	[illegible]
[illegible]	[illegible]	[illegible]	[illegible]	[illegible]	[illegible]	[illegible]	[illegible]	[illegible]	
[illegible]	Do.	[illegible]	[illegible]	[illegible]	[illegible]	[illegible]	[illegible]	[illegible]	
[illegible]	[illegible]	[illegible]	[illegible]	[illegible]	[illegible]	Do.	[illegible]	[illegible]	
[illegible]	[illegible]	[illegible]	[illegible]	[illegible]	[illegible]	Do.	[illegible]	[illegible]	

[illegible]	[illegible]	[illegible]	[illegible]
[illegible]	[illegible]	[illegible]	[illegible]
[illegible]	[illegible]	[illegible]	[illegible]
[illegible]	[illegible]	[illegible]	Do.
[illegible]	[illegible]	[illegible]	[illegible]
[illegible]	[illegible]	[illegible]	[illegible]
[illegible]	[illegible]	[illegible]	[illegible]
[illegible]	[illegible]	[illegible]	[illegible]
[illegible]	[illegible]	[illegible]	[illegible]
[illegible]	[illegible]	[illegible]	[illegible]
[illegible]	[illegible]	[illegible]	Do.
[illegible]	[illegible]	[illegible]	[illegible]
[illegible]	[illegible]	[illegible]	Do.

No. 7.—Union Officers' Superannuation.—Statement of Allowances under the Superannuation Acts in force during any portion of the year ended [illegible] September, [illegible]; showing also the cases in which the Allowances had terminated during the year. (In continuation of Statement in the [illegible] Report of the Local Government Board (Ireland), [illegible], Appendix D, No. 7)—continued.

[illegible]	[illegible]	[illegible]	[illegible]	[illegible]	[illegible]	[illegible]	[illegible]	[illegible]	[illegible]
							£ s. d.	£ s. d.	
[illegible]	Cork,	[illegible]	[illegible]	[illegible]	[illegible]	Infirmity of body	[illegible]	[illegible]	
[illegible]	Do.	[illegible]	[illegible]	[illegible]	[illegible]	Permanent infirmity of body.	[illegible]	[illegible]	
[illegible]	Do.	[illegible]	[illegible]	[illegible]	[illegible]	Do.	[illegible]	[illegible]	
[illegible]	Do.	[illegible]	[illegible]	[illegible]	[illegible]	Old age	[illegible]	[illegible]	
[illegible]	Do.	[illegible]	[illegible]	[illegible]	[illegible]	Permanent infirmity of body.	[illegible]	[illegible]	
[illegible]	[illegible]	[illegible]	[illegible]	[illegible]	[illegible]	Old age	[illegible]	[illegible]	

[illegible]	[illegible]	[illegible]	[illegible]
[illegible]	[illegible]	[illegible] of [illegible]	[illegible]
[illegible]	[illegible]	[illegible] of [illegible]	[illegible]
[illegible]	[illegible]	Do.	[illegible]
[illegible]	[illegible]	Do.	[illegible]
[illegible]	[illegible]	[illegible] of [illegible]	[illegible]
[illegible]	[illegible]	Do.	[illegible]
[illegible]	[illegible]	[illegible] of [illegible]	[illegible]
[illegible]	[illegible]	[illegible]	[illegible]
[illegible]	[illegible]	[illegible]	[illegible]
[illegible]	[illegible]	Do.	[illegible]

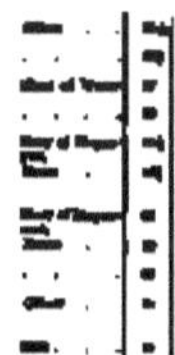

[illegible]	[illegible]	[illegible]	[illegible]	[illegible]
[illegible]	[illegible]	[illegible]	[illegible]	Do.
[illegible]	[illegible]	[illegible]	[illegible]	Do.
[illegible]	[illegible]	[illegible]	[illegible]	[illegible]
[illegible]	[illegible]	[illegible]	[illegible]	Do.
[illegible]	[illegible]	[illegible]	[illegible]	[illegible]
[illegible]	[illegible]	[illegible]	[illegible]	[illegible]
[illegible]	[illegible]	[illegible]	[illegible]	Do.
[illegible]	[illegible]	[illegible]	[illegible]	[illegible]
[illegible]	[illegible]	[illegible]	[illegible]	[illegible]
[illegible]	[illegible]	[illegible]	[illegible]	[illegible]
[illegible]	[illegible]	[illegible]	[illegible]	[illegible]
[illegible]	[illegible]	[illegible]	[illegible]	[illegible]
[illegible]	[illegible]	[illegible]	[illegible]	[illegible]
[illegible]	[illegible]	[illegible]	[illegible]	Do.
[illegible]	[illegible]	[illegible]	[illegible]	Do.
[illegible]	[illegible]	[illegible]	[illegible]	[illegible]
[illegible]	[illegible]	[illegible]	[illegible]	[illegible]
[illegible]	[illegible]	[illegible]	[illegible]	[illegible]
[illegible]	[illegible]	[illegible]	[illegible]	[illegible]

APPENDIX E.

TABULAR RETURNS IN CONNECTION WITH RELIEF UNDER THE MEDICAL CHARITIES ACT.

[NOTE.—In this series of Tables, the Unions are classed in the Counties and Provinces in which the chief or central place of the respective Unions is situate; but many of the Unions comprise parts of more than one County or Province. The total Population of the Unions in the respective Counties and Provinces, as arranged in the Summary of Table No. 2, does not, therefore, agree with the summaries of those Counties and Provinces in the Census Returns. An Index of the Dispensary Districts is annexed (No. 8), showing the name of the Union in which each District is situate, and referring to the table and page in which the particulars relating to each District are to be found.]

Table No. 1.

Statement of Alterations in Dispensary Districts of Unions in Ireland (arranged in Provinces and Counties) according to the Orders issued in pursuance of sec. 6 of 14 and 15 Vic., cap. 68:—(*from the completion of Table No. 1, Appendix B, in the Fifteenth Annual Report of the Local Government Board to 25th March,* 1888).

Name of Union.	Names of Dispensary Districts.	[illegible]	[illegible]	Number of Apothecaries.	Number of Midwives.	Date of Order.
Column 1.	2.	3.	4.	5.	6.	7.
PROVINCE OF ULSTER.						
County of Cavan.						
Cavan, . . .	Cavan, ...	29	–	–	–	21st April, 1887.
County of Tyrone.						
Cookstown, . . .	Stewartstown, .	17	–	–	–	18th April, 1887.
PROVINCE OF MUNSTER.						
County of Cork.						
Cork, . . .	Queenstown, . .	–	–	1*	–	9th April, 1887.
Do., . . .	Cork, . . .	–	–	2*	–	11th May,
Fermoy, . . .	Ballyhooly, . .	–	–	–	1	20th March, 1888.
County of Tipperary.						
Roscrea, . . .	Roscrea, ...	27	–	–	–	29th April, 1887.
PROVINCE OF LEINSTER.						
County of Dublin.						

STATEMENT of ALTERATIONS in DISPENSARY DISTRICTS—*continued.*

NAME OF UNION.	NAMES OF DISPENSARY DISTRICTS.	No. of Members of Committees of Management.	No. of Medical Officers to Dispensary Districts.	Number of Apothecaries.	Number of Midwives.	Date of Order.
Column 1.	2.	3.	4.	5.	6.	7.
PROVINCE OF LEINSTER—*continued.*						
COUNTY OF MEATH.						
TRIM, ...	Innfield, ...	–	–	–	1	18th July, 1887.
PROVINCE OF CONNAUGHT.						
COUNTY OF MAYO.						
BELMULLET, . . .	Bangor, ...	19	–	–	–	17th August, 1887.
COUNTY OF SLIGO.						
SLIGO, ...	Sligo, ...	–	–	1[a]	–	19th May, 1887.
Do., ...	Ballymote, ...	–	–	–	1	31st December, 1887.

a The Order in this case provides that the person to be appointed Apothecary in pursuance of the Order already existing, may be either an Apothecary or a Pharmaceutical Chemist.

SUMMARY OF DISPENSARY DISTRICTS, ACCORDING TO TABLE No. 1, APPENDIX E, OF PREVIOUS REPORT, AS ALTERED BY THE FOREGOING TABLE UP TO THE 25TH MARCH, 1888.

PROVINCES.	Number of Unions.	Number of Dispensary Districts.	Number of Electoral Divisions.	Population 1881.	Area in Statute Acres.	Poor Law Valuation, 29th Sept., 1887.	Number of Medical Officers under Table 1 Loans.	Number of Apothecaries.	Number of Midwives.
Column 1.	2.	3.	4.	5.	6.	7.	8.	9.	10.
						£			
ULSTER, .	44	214	879	1,743,075	5,483,201	4,368,331	235	8	88
MUNSTER, .	50	206	1,039	1,331,115	6,067,723	3,444,270	231	21	34
LEINSTER, .	39	202	938	1,278,989	4,876,918	4,746,513	228	8	142
CONNAUGHT, .	28	98	588	821,657	4,392,086	1,364,123	114	3	27
Total, Ireland,	161	720	3,444	5,174,836	20,819,928	13,917,569	808	40	311

[illegible] 156

No. 3.—Prescribing and Relief Registers.—Lists, in pursuance of § 20 of the Medical Charities Act (14 & 15 Vic., c. 68), of all Dispensary Districts in the several Unions in Ireland (arranged in Provinces and Counties);—showing the Number of Dispensaries in each, and the Expenses of each Dispensary District for the Year ended 29th September, 1857; with a Return,—for the Year ended 29th September, 1857,—of the [illegible] of Cases of Medical Relief afforded to Patients at Dispensaries and at their own Homes, respectively; the Number of Tickets for Medical Relief [illegible] by the Committee of Management, under § 9 of the Act; Number of Cases of Vaccination; Number of Dangerous Lunatics certified; of Patients attended by [illegible], &c.

[illegible] Table, No. 3.

[illegible]

Name of Union.	Name of Dispensary District.	[illegible]	[illegible]	Expenses of Year ended 29th September, 1857.	[illegible]
[illegible]	[illegible]	[illegible]	[illegible]	[illegible]	[illegible]

[illegible]

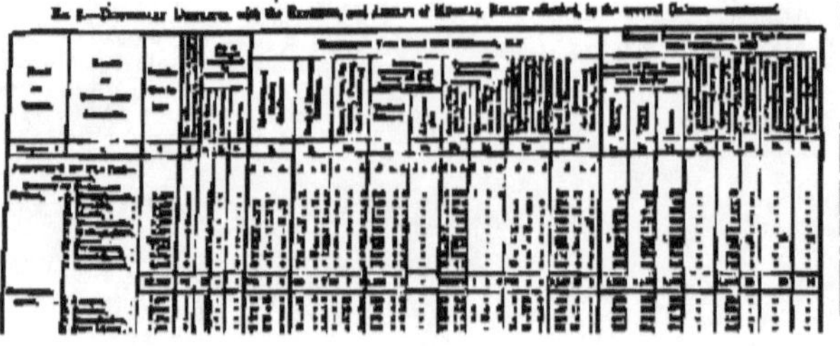

No. 8.—[illegible] Districts, with the Expenses, and Amount of [illegible] Relief afforded, in the several Unions—continued.

[illegible]

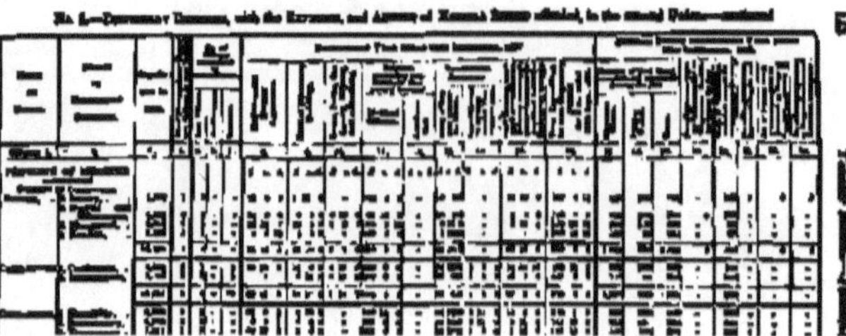

[illegible]

[illegible]
[illegible]

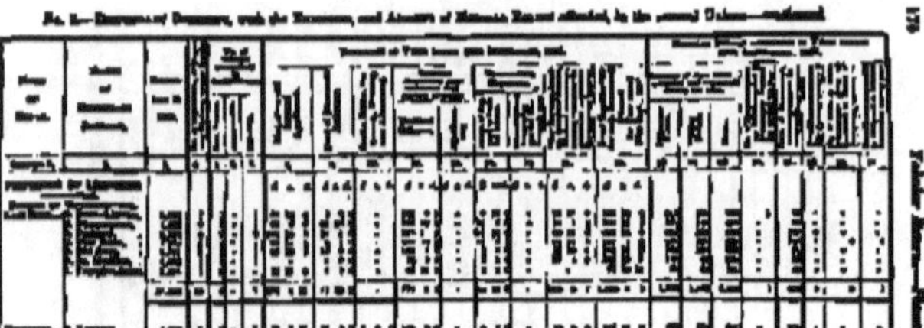

SUMMARY OF FOREGOING TABLE, No. 1.

[illegible]

No. 3.—General Summary of previous Tables, in Provinces;—containing, 1.
Dispensary Districts formed under § 6 of the Medical Charities Act, 14 &
of Dispensaries, Officers, &c.;—2. Financial Statement; showing the
1886, to 29th September, 1887;—and 3. Relief Return; showing the
Homes, respectively; the Number of Cases in which Tickets for Medical
Vaccination performed; Number of Cases of Dangerous Lunatics certified;
year ended 30th September, 1887.

STATISTICAL STATEMENT; showing the number of Unions, Electoral Divisions, and
15 Vic., c. 68; the total and average Population, Area, and Valuation; Number
Expenditure under the Medical Charities Act for the year from 29th September,
Number of Cases of Medical Relief afforded at the Dispensaries and at the Patients'
Relief have been Cancelled by the Dispensary Committees; the Number of Cases of
Number of Patients attended at Bridewells or Houses of Correction, &c.; during the

LEINSTER.		CONNAUGHT.		TOTAL for IRELAND.		AVERAGE.		
						Per Union.	Per Dispensary District.	Per Medical Officer.
6.	7.	8.	9.	10.	11.	12.	13.	14.
. .	1,078,600	. .	321,637	. .	6,174,896	80,143	7,187	6,416
. .	4,876,918	. .	4,[illegible],054	. .	20,819,025	180,316	20,917	—
. .	£4,749,461	. .	£1,388,423	. .	£13,617,078	£80,445	£19,320	—
. .	39	. .	25	. .	161	—	—	—
. .	137	. .	465	. .	6,444	81	5	6
. .	104	. .	95	. .	720	4	—	—
. .	225	. .	163	. .	3,111	7	—	—
. .	227	. .	114	. .	507	6	—	—
. .	14	. .	8	. .	41	—	—	—
. .	142	. .	26	. .	309	3	—	—
£		£		£		£ s.	£ s.	£ s.
7,117	. .	4,517	. .	25,465	. .	164 8	36 15	39 16
2,031	. .	1,006	. .	6,213	. .	61 16	11 19	—
631	. .	103	. .	1,167	. .	7 7	1 13	—
20,718	. .	12,165	. .	80,167	. .	533 9	123 18	110 8
1,271	. .	152	. .	2,429	. .	—	—	80 0
7,281	. .	1,067	. .	10,813	. .	64 1	14 6	—
8,718	. .	2,549	. .	30,230	. .	125 1	47 18	—
. .	£48,031	. .	£23,184	. .	£169,578	£853 14	£316 18	—
147,703	. .	51,229	. .	406,692	. .	2,476	586	604
59,177	. .	15,371	. .	172,307	. .	1,019	241	219
. .	201,682	. .	68,900	. .	887,240	8,606	606	718
. .	46	. .	29	. .	271	—	—	—
. .	81,635	. .	16,886	. .	96,190	—	—	—
. .	610	. .	197	. .	1,625	—	—	—
. .	101	. .	63	. .	362	—	—	—

No. 4.—Vaccination:—Summary of the Number of Persons Vaccinated in the Workhouses and Auxiliary Establishments of the several Unions in Ireland by the Medical Officers of those Institutions; and of the Number Vaccinated in the several Dispensary Districts, by the Medical Officers thereof, in the Year ended 30th September, 1887:—abstracted from Returns made by the respective Medical Officers.

Provinces.	No. Vaccinated in Workhouses by Medical Officers thereof.			No. of Cases Vaccinated by Medical Officers of Dispensary Districts.	Total Number returned in Columns 4 and 5.	Provinces.
	Successful Cases.	Unsuccessful Cases.	Total.			
1.	2.	3.	4.	5.	6.	
Ulster, . . .	306	31	337	34,330	34,667	Ulster.
Munster, . . .	279	17	296	25,244	25,540	Munster.
Leinster, . . .	318	3	631	21,025	21,956	Leinster.
Connaught, . . .	66	–	66	15,380	15,446	Connaught.
Total, . .	000	51	1,020	00,450	07,509	

No. 5.—Number of Cases of Scarlatina, Smallpox, and Fever, reported by Medical Officers of Dispensary Districts in Ireland, as having been attended in the Quarters ended 31st December, 1886, 31st March, 30th June, and 30th September, 1887.

Provinces.	Quarters ended	Scarlatina.	Smallpox.	Fever.
Ulster, . .	December 31st, 1886, . .	347	1	[illegible]
	March 31st, 1887, . .	168	–	[illegible]
	June 30th, 1887, . .	185	5	[illegible]
	September 30th, 1887, . .	175	5	[illegible]
Munster, . .	December 31st, 1886, . .	235	1	[illegible]
	March 31st, 1887, . .	199	1	[illegible]
	June 30th, 1887, . .	170	1	[illegible]
	September 30th, 1887, . .	98	2	[illegible]
Leinster, . .	December 31st, 1886, . .	011	–	303
	March 31st, 1887, . .	304	–	315
	June 30th, 1887, . .	471	1	411
	September 30th, 1887, . .	027	1	410
Connaught, . .	December 31st, 1886, . .	10	–	155
	March 31st, 1887, . .	15	–	184
	June 30th, 1887, . .	52	–	[illegible]
	September 30th, 1887, . .	34	–	[illegible]
Summary.				
Ireland, . .	December 31st, 1886, . .	1,293	2	1,110
	March 31st, 1887, . .	705	1	[illegible]
	June 30th, 1887, . .	887	7	[illegible]
	September 30th, 1887, . .	934	6	[illegible]
	Total, ...	3,819	16	[illegible]

No. 6.—INDEX LIST of DISPENSARY DISTRICTS, with NAMES of UNIONS in which they are situate, and REFERENCES to PAGES in which the Districts are to be found in the Appendix.

[continued.

Name of Dispensary District.	Union in which situate.	Reference to Dispensary District Tables, App. E, No. 1.	Reference to Dispensary Tables, App. E, No. 2.
		Page	Page
Bl[illegible]stown,	Balrothery,	–	176
Blackrock and Stillorgan,	Rathdown,	–	167
Blackwatertown,	Armagh,	–	149
Blanchardstown & Castleknock,	North Dublin,	–	169
Blarney,	Cork,	–	158
Blessington and Ballymore,	Naas,	–	169
Boherboy,	Kanturk,	–	159
Borris,	Carlow,	–	168
Borris-in-Ossory,	Roscrea,	–	174
Borrisokane,	Borrisokane,	–	16[illegible]
Borrisoleigh,	Thurles,	–	162
Bournay,	Roscrea,	–	174
Boyle,	Boyle,	–	179
Bray and Rathmichael,	Rathdown,	–	167
Brideswell,	Athlone,	–	173
Bridgetown,	Limerick,	–	163
Bridgetown,	Wexford,	–	171
Broadford,	Newcastle,	–	163
Broadway,	Wexford,	–	171
Brookeborough,	Lisnaskea,	–	155
Brosna,	Tralee,	–	161
Broughshane,	Ballymena,	–	147
Bruff,	Kilmallock,	–	167
Bruree,	Kilmallock,	–	162
[illegible],	Kildare,	–	1[illegible]
[illegible],	Longford,	–	178
Buncrana,	Inishowen,	–	156
Bunmahon,	Kilmacthomas,	–	165
Burt,	Londonderry,	–	153
Bushmills,	Coleraine,	–	153
Buttevant,	Mallow,	–	158
Cahir,	Cahersiveen,	–	161
Cahir,	Clogheen,	–	164
Caherconlish,	Limerick,	–	163
Caledon,	Armagh,	–	149
Callan,	Callan,	–	168
Camolin,	Gorey,	–	173
[illegible],	[illegible],	–	160
Cappagh,	Tipperary,	–	163
Cappoquin,	Lismore,	–	165
Carn[illegible],	Londonderry,	–	153
Carlingford,	Dundalk,	–	171
Carlow,	Carlow,	–	166
Carndonagh,	Inishowen,	–	156
Carney,	Sligo,	–	168
Carrick,	Glenties,	–	160
Carrickbyrne,	New Ross,	–	175
Carrickfergus,	Larne,	–	147
Carrickmacross,	Carrickmacross,	–	161
Carrick-on-Suir,	Carrick-on-Suir,	–	160
Carrigaholt,	Kilrush,	–	167
Carrigaline,	Cork,	–	158
Carrig[illegible],	Kinsale,	–	158
Carrigallen,	Mohill,	–	177
Carrignavar,	Cork,	–	158
Cashel,	Cashel,	–	163
Castlebar,	Castlebar,	–	178
Castlebellingham,	Ardee,	–	170
Castleblayney,	Castleblayney,	–	164
Castlecomer,	Castlecomer,	–	168
Castlederg and Killeter,	Castlederg,	–	155
Castledermot,	Athy,	–	167
Castle Finn,	Strabane,	–	159
Castlegregory,	Dingle,	–	161
Castle Island,	Tralee,	–	160
Castlemaine,	Tralee,	–	160
Castlemartyr,	Midleton,	–	160
Castleplunket,	Castlerea,	–	179
Castlepollard,	Delvin,	–	180
Castle Quarter,	Ballymoney,	–	147
Castlerea,	Castlerea,	–	179
Castlereagh,	Belfast,	–	147
Castleshane,	Monaghan,	–	154
Castletown,	Abbeyleix,	–	173
Castletown,	Castletown,	–	159
Castletown,	Croom,	–	163
Castletown,	Navan,	–	171
Castletown Geoghegan,	Mullingar,	–	173
Cavan,	Cavan,	146	172
Celbridge,	Celbridge,	–	167
Charleville,	Kilmallock,	–	163
Church Hill,	Ballyshannon,	–	153
Churchhill,	Letterkenny,	–	154
Clane and Timahoe North,	Naas,	–	169
Clara,	Tullamore,	–	180
Claremorris,	Claremorris,	–	178
Clarina,	Limerick,	–	163
Clashmore,	Youghal,	–	161
Claudy,	Londonderry,	–	153
Clifden,	Clifden,	–	176
Clogh,	Ballymena,	–	147
Cloghan,	Stranorlar,	–	154
Clogheen,	Clogheen,	–	161
Clogher,	Clogher,	–	155
Cloghjordan,	Borrisokane,	–	163
Clonakilty,	Clonakilty,	–	158
Clonaslee,	Mountmellick,	–	173
Clonavaddy,	Dungannon,	–	156
Clonbrock,	Mount Bellew,	–	176
Clondalkin,	South Dublin,	–	167
Clonelly,	Irvinestown,	–	155
Clones,	Clones,	–	154
Clonmany,	Inishowen,	–	156
Clonmel & St. Mary's,	Clonmel,	–	164
Clonmellon,	Delvin,	–	173
Clonmoyle,	Macroom,	–	159
Clonroche,	Enniscorthy,	–	175
Clontarf and Howth,	North Dublin,	–	166
Clonygowan,	Mountmellick,	–	173
Cloonbur,	Oughterard,	–	177
Clough,	Downpatrick,	–	151
Cloyne,	Midleton,	–	160
Coagh,	Cookstown,	–	155
Coal Island,	Dungannon,	–	156
Coleraine,	Coleraine,	–	153
Collon,	Ardee,	–	170
Collooney,	Sligo,	–	168
Comber,	Newtownards,	–	150
Cong,	Ballinrobe,	–	178
Connor,	Antrim,	–	147
Cookstown,	Cookstown,	–	155
[illegible],	Limerick,	–	163
Coolaney,	Tobercurry,	–	168
Coolattin and Clonegall,	Shillelagh,	–	170
Coole,	Granard,	–	170
Coolgreany,	Gorey,	–	173

[continued.

[continued.

[continued

[continued.

Dublin: Printed for Her Majesty's Stationery Office,
By Alex. Thom & Co. (Limited), 87, 88, & 89, Abbey-street,
The Queen's Printing Office.

www.ingramcontent.com/pod-product-compliance
Lightning Source LLC
Chambersburg PA
CBHW020932180426
43192CB00036B/732

* 9 7 8 3 7 4 2 8 1 1 2 0 2 *